KATHERINE THOMSON began in theatre with ATYP in 1969. An actor for fifteen years, she was a founding member of Wollongong's Theatre South performing in fifteen productions over four years. In 1982 she wrote *A Change in the Weather* about Wollongong women at work performed at the 1982 Women & Arts Festival. Her next play, *Tonight We Anchor in Twofold Bay*, toured the South Coast before a season at STC's Wharf Studio. In 1987 Magpie Theatre Company of the STCSA commissioned *A Sporting Chance* which has been performed by leading TIE companies throughout Australia. She then wrote *Darlinghurst Nights* based on the light verse of Kenneth Slessor with music by Max Lambert as part of the STC's tenth birthday season in 1988; a radio version has since been broadcast by Radio National. In 1988 with a Writer's Development Grant from the Australia Council she wrote *Diving for Pearls* which premiered at the MTC in 1991 and was also produced that year by Belvoir St; 1992 productions include the STCSA as well as Theatre South in conjunction with the Riverina Theatre Company. As an actor her most recent work has been in STC's *An Ideal Husband* and the TV series *The Private War of Lucinda Smith*. In 1990 she was Writer-In-Residence for Deck Chair Theatre Company in Fremantle and returned to write *Barmaids* which premiered there in November 1991.

With thanks to Bob, and the Timbs family of Dapto.

DIVING
for PEARLS

KATHERINE THOMSON

CURRENCY PRESS · SYDNEY

CURRENCY PLAYS
General Editor: Katharine Brisbane

First published in 1992 by
Currency Press Ltd
PO Box 452, Paddington NSW 2021, Australia

National Library of Australia
Cataloguing-in-Publication data
    Thomson, Katherine, 1955-
      Diving for pearls.

    ISBN 0 86819 323 2.

    I. Title.

A822.3

Printed by Australian Print Group, Maryborough, Vic.
Cover design by Trevor Hood
Cover photo shows Robyn Nevin, Jeanette Cronin and Marshall Napier
Cover photo by Tracey Moffatt

Australia Council
for the Arts

Publication of this title was assisted by the Australia Council, the Federal Government's arts funding and advisory body.

CONTENTS

PHOTO ACKNOWLEDGMENTS: p.15 Above: Robyn Nevin as Barbara and Marshall Napier as Den in the Belvoir St Theatre production, 1991. Below: Marshall Napier and Robyn Nevin. Photographer: Philip Le Masurier. p.29 Above: Robyn Nevin as Barbara and Pat Bishop as Marge in the Belvoir St production. Below: Marshall Napier and Robyn Nevin. p.47 Above: Tammy McCarthy as Verge and Peter Cummins as Den in the MTC production, 1991. Below: Denis Moore as Ron and Peter Cummins as Den in the same production. Photographer: Jeff Busby. p.57 Jeanette Cronin as Verge in the Belvoir St production. p.81 Above: Peter Cummins as Den and Belinda Davey as Barbara in the MTC production. Below: Peter Cummins, Belinda Davey and Tammy McCarthy. p.85 Above: Marshall Napier and Jeanette Cronin in the Belvoir St production. Below: Belinda Davey and Peter Cummins in the MTC production.

The author would like to thank the Literature Board of the Australia Council and Playworks Women Writers' Workshop.

High Hopes are Not Enough

Di Kelly

At the beginning of 1982 over twenty-one thousand people were employed at the Port Kembla steelworks near Wollongong in NSW. Within eighteen months this number had fallen to under fourteen thousand, and that decline continued for a decade. Ten years later there were fewer than eight thousand at the same plant. Many more thousands of jobs in the firms which served the steelworks have also disappeared. And the lives of those thousands who lost their jobs or resigned before it was too late would never be the same. Yet the experience of Wollongong was not unique.

From the mid-1970s the world market for steel became ever more competitive. On the one hand products such as plastic and aluminium were competing with steel. On the other hand former customers in newly industrialising countries like Korea, Taiwan and Brazil were now competitors with the old steel producing countries in Europe, North America and Australia. In industrial regions throughout the world, there were crises of mass reductions in employment and in many there was very little in the way of alternative employment for the redundant male workers. So sang Billy Joel in his 1981 hit song about American steel towns and the closure of the giant Bethlehem steelworks (which he called *Allentown*):

> they're closing all the factories down
> Out in Bethlehem they're killing time,
> Filling out forms
> standing in line.

So the experience of those in this play is not just some rare Australian occurrence, and the fears and problems of Den and Barbara are the same as those that existed in the old industrial cities in the U.S.A, the United Kingdom and throughout Europe. In Australia, like many countries in Europe, employees were not simply laid off. There was redundancy pay, or special severance pay for those who resigned voluntarily. Many of them rested their hope in the possibility that they could use their severance pay to start a small business, or gain new skills for new occupations.

So Christmas 1983 in the steel and coal towns of Australia was a strange time of fear and spending, when people in safe jobs crossed to the other side of the street to avoid those who might have lost or left their jobs; and those who no longer had jobs spent their money in the hope that jobs might miraculously appear. Then there were those who were not quite sure that they would still have a job by the following Christmas, nor what they would do if indeed they did lose their jobs. A lifetime working in a steel plant or a contract engineering firm does not make for portable skills. Many of the employees who resigned or were retrenched were unready and untrained for other sorts of work. Like Den who stays with his job for as long as he can in the hope that things might come good, they were often doomed to disappointment. But they stayed and hoped for better things, or tried to set up small businesses or trained for different jobs.

But the problem was that new occupations required new industries and investors were wary. Media stories of industrial cities almost always exaggerate the militancy of the workers, or tell tales of their conservative work habits. On the television news, stories of steel towns are almost always represented through pictures of chimneys, spouting what looks like plumes of smoke. The fact that those plumes are nothing more than steam would spoil a good story, and so the public image of steel towns remained flawed and the investors stayed away.

Many of the workers were migrants who had been coming to Australia since the 1940s in search of a better life. In the

1980s, they had to contend not only with increasingly inappropriate skills specific to old technology of heavy industry or steel production, but with the language and cultural differences found in a society which mostly pays only lip-service to multiculturalism.

It was worse for migrant women. Traditionally, industrial cities have woefully few jobs for women and in relatively recent cities like Wollongong, the situation was aggravated by the absence of other industries. Like Topsy, Wollongong had just grown from a small industrial centre, surrounded by a multiplicity of mining villages prior to World War II, to a burgeoning unplanned, under-resourced city in the 1960s and 1970s, its growth in population outpacing the social and economic infrastructure needed to support such a city. To be sure, women with few recognised skills could work in clothing factories, with Draconian working conditions easily enforced because of the vast pool of unemployed women ready to replace those who questioned the rules, but there were only a few of even these undesirable sorts of jobs. There were office jobs too, but not many. So there were few jobs for women, but especially migrant women. Barbara's desperate attempts to change her appearance and her vowels underline the even greater problems which would face migrant women who had to contend with language difficulties and prejudice, probably not in that order. In an international downturn in the market, those with least skills, and the least portable skills are the most vulnerable.

But life in the steel towns is one of contradictions, as we see in the play. Coal and steel sandwiched between superb beaches and miles of rainforest. Heavy industry is not pretty, but it is surprisingly limited in its impact on the environment. The worst pollution may come from the nearby metropolis. Within a mile or two of the engineering district, the new international resort can justifiably portray flawless images of sun, sea and sand. There is no dirt, no dust, no smell of industry.

It is not surprising then, that when the steel cities reeled from the shocks of workforce reductions, they looked to these features as possible alternatives to the making of steel and the hewing of coal. Gradually, over the years following the first major reductions, the local authorities, commercial organisations and trade unions cajoled and enticed new industries in the hope that never again would the town put all its economic reliance on a single industry.

Despite all the best efforts, however, recovery was not fast enough and there were never enough jobs to go around – particularly for those with fewest modern skills or vulnerable in other respects, such as older workers, younger workers, women, migrants, aborigines – so many of whom wanted to work but for whom there were just no jobs. And then came the recession of the 1990s...

Department of Economics
University of Wollongong, 1992

The Audience Wants to Worry

Paul Thompson

In the last decade of the twentieth century it is not easy to explain why there should be so much drama in the world and so little of any consequence on the stage. Perhaps some playwrights offer light relief in troubled times, whilst others, overwhelmed by the magnitude of events, choose silence. Meanwhile, the audience that seeks engagement in the public debate turns to television, the docu-drama, rap music or the stand-up comic. The theatre is rarely where one goes to hear the news in Australia in the 1990s.

Diving for Pearls is an exception. It is a courageous and thrilling attempt to unite public issues and private concerns. The play captures the nineties with the same cunning that the *Summer of the Seventeenth Doll, The Shifting Heart* and *Don's Party* captured their respective periods. *Diving for Pearls* is a precious contribution to a noble tradition of dramatic writing in Australia.

Long before the play's first production in Melbourne, Katherine Thomson and the director, Ros Horin, asked me to join them as the dramaturg. I was immediately attracted by the subject matter of the play and the authenticity of the treatment. I felt that the writer knew this world and described it with authority.

Whenever I assess a new work, my first consideration is – necessity. Is this a story that needs to be told? Is there an audience that needs to hear it? My next concern is the element of anxiety – does the theme touch upon a common anxiety? Whether one loves or hates the films *Fatal Attraction* and *Home*

Alone it is clear that the former touches a male anxiety and the latter plays upon the parental fear of leaving a child in danger. A classic example is the Olivier film of Henry V. In 1944 that was the story that needed to be told. It reflected the anxiety of the time. Anxiety can also generate a strong narrative through the skilful combination of hope and fear. We should hope he gets the girl, but fear he won't. We should hope the cop catches the criminal, but fear she won't. My emphasis on the anxiety principle is based upon my observation that people go to the movies and the theatre, not as they might claim, for a good time, but actually because they want to worry. This applies equally to John Cleese comedies and Jacobean tragedies. It applies to creation myths, fairy tales and bedtime stories. The audience wants anxiety.

Diving for Pearls is a story that needs to be told. The play addresses our current fears and insecurities. We are all afraid of the economic recession, the changing world, getting older and being alone. *Diving for Pearls* offers a wonderful group of characters. We identify with their hopes and fears as they set out on their respective journeys through the play. We hope that Barbara will make it, we fear that she won't.

Katherine Thomson is a wonderful craftsperson, she is a natural dramatist and a writer of memorable dialogue. Her work is informed by a generosity of spirit and an unsentimental respect for the dignity of ordinary people.

As her dramaturg my principle function was to act as a sounding board, to reinforce her confidence and to encourage her to trust her own voice.

With such a talented writer it would seem reasonable to question the value of the dramaturg. In the case of *Diving for Pearls* I am tempted to confess that the dramaturg was as many people already suspect - just the German word for job creation. But in these terrible times who could complain about any job creation scheme?

Australian Film, Television and Radio School, 1992

Diving for Pearls was first performed by the Melbourne Theatre Company at the Geelong Performing Arts Centre on the 22nd March, 1991 followed by a season at the MTC's Russell Street Theatre, with the following cast:

BARBARA	Belinda Davey
DEN	Peter Cummins
RON	Denis Moore
MARGE	Jan Friel
VERGE	Tammy McCarthy

Dramaturg (Playworks), Paul Thompson
Director, Ros Horin
Designer, Richard Roberts
Lighting designer, Jamieson Lewis
Music, Martin Friedel
Production co-ordinator, Ian Cookesley
Stage manager, Greg Diamantis
Assistant stage manager, Jamie Ivarsen
Sound recording/lighting operator, Kerry Saxby
Student director, Jemima Mead

CHARACTERS

DEN, in his late forties, early fifties. DEN has been very much in love with BARBARA. He is a loner, shy. If you asked him what he'd been doing for the last twenty years he would probably be able to answer you in one sentence. He and BARBARA have not seen each other for about four months, and this was his first love affair. He is still unsure as to what went wrong, apart from the fact that it was never consummated.

RON, an industrial consultant, and DEN's brother-in-law. A couple of years younger than Den. He and Den grew up in the same industrial suburb.

BARBARA, close to forty. BARBARA is overweight, she has not looked after herself, and is going through a rougher patch than usual. She has worked in a clothing factory since the age of fourteen and is accomplished at standing up for herself. While she eschews self pity, there is a vulnerability to her, despite her brittleness.

MARJ, BARBARA's sister, a few years older than BARBARA. She has cultivated an accent which approaches educated Australian, she has also cultivated a soft voice – which she can use like a laser if necessary.

VERGE, twenty-one, BARBARA's daughter. She is mildly intellectually disabled, having suffered from a lack of oxygen at birth. She may have a slight physical deformity. She concentrates hard when talking to someone, and her voice is slightly less modulated than normal. At times she has unusual tempo/rhythms. She is neatly dressed, but is dressed much older than is appropriate for her age – twenty. She has spent most of her life in a home, from a young age she was prone to self-directed aggression, which she now has under control. She would probably like to leap out of her own body. She prides herself on her acute judgement and her ability to stand up for herself.

SETTING

A coastal industrial city in contemporary Australia. The play takes place over a period of approximately seven months.

AUTHOR'S NOTE

The play takes place in many different locations. The set should be multilevel, abstract and evoke a feeling of both coastal and industrial landscapes. There should be multifunctional areas where props could be placed to suggest internal and external worlds. There could be crevices in which people might stand, in which DEN could shovel, for instance, and which might suggest shifting land. A hill looks onto DEN's suburb. Just behind this, coalwash is being dumped, as fill for a park.

There should be some objects in the space. A tuba, a model railway or part of a railway. Protuberances might become desks, beauty tables etc.

Note (p.33) If it is not possible to lower a noose into the space, then RON can storm on and throw it across the space, as if he has just pulled it down. In which case the following dialogue occurs at the beginning of the scene.

RON: Jesus Christ.

> [*He immediately goes to pick it up, turning to a group of unseen men as he does.*]

Thanks for this. Very subtle. Very clever. Got the message. [*To himself*] That's right, all I'm doing is just jerking you all off. . .

> [DEN *approaches, as is etc. The scene then continues with* DEN's *'that was a bit rough'. . . etc. Except that* DEN's *line, 'I'll do that' will become, 'I'll take care of that'.*]

ACT ONE

BARBARA *has been running. She arrives up on the hill. She stumbles, it is uneven and rocky. She takes off her shoe and examines it. There is a hole right through to the cardboard inner-sole.*

She takes a cigarette out of a packet, but after three or four attempts, it is obvious that the lighter is not going to work. She throws it behind her and finds a book of matches in her bag. Only one match is left however, and she almost burns her finger, then it disintegrates without lighting the cigarette.

The funeral which she has just attended is the final straw in a long line of events. Still no luck with the cigarette. She wears a uniform dress with a cardigan over it.

BARBARA: Unbelievable. . . honestly to god . . .

> [*She continues to fumble with the shoe.*]

Don't tell me funerals aren't a waste of time. Felt like seeing two people in the entire church and one of them was in a box.

> [*She searches again for a match, then looks down towards the church.*]

And don't put yourself out. Don't bother getting a person's name right — bloody priests, probably didn't slip him enough. John this. John that. Jacko. Jacko. I didn't know who he was talking about. Not a mention that he hung himself, of course. Start up a trend.

> [*Sound of a coal truck going by. Later we hear it returning.*]

You live next door to someone eighteen years, you'd know if anyone ever called him John. Which they didn't.

[DEN *arrives. He has followed her up the hill, unsure as to whether he should have come. She acknowledges him; she thought he would probably show up.*]

Well, you won't have a light.

[*There is the sound of a coal truck and they wait for it to pass.*]

I thought that was you. Thought that was you at the back of the church.

DEN: Yes. [*Nervous smile*] So. . .

BARBARA: Then I thought it wasn't.

[*Pause*]

I mean I didn't come up here expecting you to follow me. I'm not thirteen. I have been up on this hill without you you know.

DEN: Just to see how you were. Just to see how you're getting on.

BARBARA: Oh, well brilliant of course. Getting on brilliant.

DEN: Bit of a shock. [*Looking back down towards the church*] All very sudden. Heart I thought someone said. . . You wouldn't think. . .

[BARBARA *is silent, and* DEN *produces a lighter in a leather case. He gives it to her and she hangs it around her neck. Pause.*]

Didn't know if you realised you left it.

[*Pause*]

I came back from getting the chips and it was where you'd been sitting, on that bench. And of course you were. . . Quite a few months old, might be dried out by now. . .

[BARBARA *lights a cigarette.*]

You look nice.

BARBARA: Well, how was I supposed to know you'd be there. And all them. Everyone I've ever known practically, all having a gawk. God, funerals are stupid.

[*Pause*]

You wouldn't have been mates with Jacko.

DEN: Well, work – I used to see him.

BARBARA: But you wouldn't have known him. You wouldn't have played cards with him at lunch for instance.

DEN: I told you what I'm like – a quiet corner with a cowboy novel and a couple of devon sandwiches.

BARBARA: No, you'd steer clear of any trouble-makers.

DEN: Kept him pretty busy, shaking things up.

BARBARA: Someone has to.

DEN: Fills in the time.

BARBARA: Someone has to. People rely on people like him to give things a shake-up. You probably never spoke to him.

DEN: There's a lot of men in that plant.

BARBARA: Used to be.

DEN: Yes.

BARBARA: Opposite of you, he was. He didn't let that place get to him. He got to it.

[*Pause.* DEN *longs to talk to her and doesn't know what to say.* BARBARA *looks down the hill.*]

DEN: His old man knew mine. Miner's Federation. Why I came.

[*Pause*]

I was hoping I'd see you. I remembered once that you said you knew him.

BARBARA: Why that church? Very woggy if you ask me. Couldn't be woggier if they tried. [*Looking*] And that bloody mob from the Northern Beaches. [*To them*] Sorry you had to drag yourselves south of the steelworks. Still hanging round. Yap yap yap yap. All kissing each other.

[*She draws a line in the air.*]

You could divide this city in half, I reckon. They're getting everything up there. [*To* DEN] We used to feel sorry for them stuck out on bloody cliffs, living in their poky little shacks. 'Oh, Barbara, people are coming down and paying a quarter of a million dollars for our little miners' cottages!' They used to be bloody communists.

DEN: I've been thinking about you – quite a bit.

BARBARA: Shocking bloody view – look at that.

DEN: Oh well.

BARBARA: Oh well what?

DEN: No smoke from the steelworks and we'd all be in trouble. [*Slight pause*] And our joint. . . always looks bigger from up here – out there on the point. . . Never minded those roofs. That shape.

> [BARBARA *looks at him.*]

Jagged like that. You know what I mean.

BARBARA: They want to find a way to cover it all up.

DEN: Just look over it and you can see the sea. I wondered if –

> [*A coal truck. She looks down to the church.*]

BARBARA: Fifty, he was. Bugger of an age.

DEN: Same as me.

BARBARA: Bugger of an age to be retrenched.

DEN: Yeah.

BARBARA: Don't tell me the whole country didn't watch him on telly, storming Parliament House.

> [*Pause*]
>
> [*To* DEN] I bet you never even went.
>
> [*No reply from* DEN. *More proof to* BARBARA *that he is just not right for her.*]

Pride. Lifts up other people, pride. He was on every channel. And I taped it. You wouldn't still be working there except for that.

DEN: They were always going to keep fifty per cent of us.

> [*Pause*]

There's talk of running us more like a business, not so much like a government enterprise.

BARBARA: Very hopeful I don't think. Bit late for him however it goes.

DEN: Probably just a rumour.

BARBARA: And they say it doesn't affect people. I'll tell you something he told me and he never told anyone else. Oh, I suppose you think there was something funny going on.

DEN: No.

BARBARA: [*looking back down hill*] Because unlike some, I don't root my next-door neighbour, not when he's a mate. Not in my books anyway.

DEN: You could come and have a cup of tea.

BARBARA: [*continuing with what* JACKO *told her*] That three months after they gave him the boot he joins up one of those unemployment groups – this is the man who bellowed on national telly – he's in this group and he stands up, opens his mouth to say his name, bursts into tears and can't stop. And he was more determined than most. Not the type to sit around waiting for the Tai-Chi class to start. [*Looking back down the hill*] I'm not going down until they all clear off.

[*Pause*]

DEN: What I wondered was – has she gone back – to your husband?

BARBARA: And of course, he'd be down there [*The church*] Barry. Bloody twenty year old sheila dripping off his arm. Finally got on to the garbage trucks, aren't things looking up.

DEN: I thought, she's done her disappearing act on *me* this time.

BARBARA: [*still looking at the church*] I should have. I meant to just disappear. They all think I'm mad, Jacko never did. I could talk to Jacko. I said, 'Jacko, the thing is this, and I know it's happening to all of you, but Barry hasn't even had a day's work since the abattoirs shifted and I can't stand it. If I'd wanted a dog without a name I'd go out and buy one. And I don't mind Housing Commission, I never have, but we've all lived in each other's pockets for too long. I've won every prize at bingo, I've borrowed every decent video, and I'm starting to go off the football. And if I sew another collar and cuff on another permanent press business shirt I'll – do myself in –', and he smiled at me and said, 'Barbara, I know that feeling. Hit the toe. If I didn't have kids I'd be right behind you'. That's how I decided. Never told you why, now you know.

DEN: I didn't ask.

BARBARA: Bit mysterious. . . let you use your imagination.

DEN: I think I might have left that on the bus.

BARBARA: Not as if I was leaving any kids, was it?

[*Pause*]

DEN: I know I shouldn't have, but I did go by the. . .

BARBARA: You can say it. The boarding house.

DEN: The boarding house. The landlady said you'd moved.

BARBARA: No. Still there. Take a lot to get me out of Buena Vista.

DEN: You can't expect things to happen all at once.

BARBARA: I do. Why shouldn't I?

[DEN *smiles*]

DEN: I thought about you a lot.

BARBARA: Well that's right. You're a thinker.

DEN: Me. I am?

[*Slight pause.* BARBARA *starts to go.*]

I did start those classes. Wanted you to know.

BARBARA: Well you had to. Can't be an unskilled labourer all your life.

DEN: Then I stopped.

[*A breeze begins to blow coalwash dust into their faces. She fishes in her bag.*]

A westerly. . Haven't had one for a while. Blowing off the top of the coalwash. Look, when you think about it, we didn't give this much of a go. Us. If you ever. . . needed anything. . . it was nice. . . something to look forward to.

[*She turns on him.*]

BARBARA: Look, I saw that coming before. Working your way up to it. Next step the cot, and once you're in that it's a very steep climb out.

[BARBARA *is trying to protect her eyes and face. Looks behind him.*]

How much more of that stuff do they want to dump? How you can stand living up here I don't know.

DEN: One house all my life, you don't ever think of moving. I mean they'll turn it into a park. . .

[*She gets out her sunglasses.*]

BARBARA: Believe it when I see the grass. Another swifty from the steelworks.

[DEN *nods.*]

I don't think this is going to get any better. Well, I don't know about you but I've had it.

[*She puts her handkerchief over her mouth and starts to move down the hill.*]

DEN: Suppose you've been seeing someone else.

BARBARA: Suppose you have.

[*And she goes.*]

The workplace, the State Engineering Works. RON, DEN'*s brother-in-law, enters.* RON *is trundling in a trolley piled high with filing boxes, books and papers and at the top a couple of concertina files. The trolley has a recalcitrant wheel, causing it to lean to one side which at times leads him around in circles. He drops some files that he is carrying under his arm, and when he stops the trolley the box at the top lurches forward and falls. Various items spill e.g. the contents of the expanding files, manila folders, transparencies.*

RON: Oh hell.

[*He decides against scooping them up, so as to preserve their alphabetical order. He puts books on the ones likely to fly away, and begins to put them back in the file.* DEN, *sweeping, on another part of the space, sees him clutching at all the papers. He is the last person he expected to see.*]

DEN: Ron?

RON: Denny!

[*It's an old joke –* RON *does the twist.*]

DEN: [*obliging*] Ronny.

RON: I thought I'll dump all this and come over to fabrication and see you – [*Looks down*] and I did.

[*He bends down to push papers back into a few more folders.* DEN *starts to help.*]

DEN: What are you doing here?

RON: [*looks up*] Bit keen, the others aren't coming in until tomorrow. [*As he picks things up*] The only one in the consultancy without an MBA from Harvard, if they saw this they'd know why. [*Looks around*] And what about this! I'm coming in the gate and I thought, they'll recognise me, ask me for the screwdrivers back. [*Looking back towards the gate*] Yes! Where you come in there used to be a flower garden. That flower garden's gone.

DEN: Can't say I remember that.

RON: Look at this place!

> [DEN *is deeply aware that he is meant to know why* RON *is here. He is in a state of suspension, seeing what clues he might pick up.*]

DEN: [*nodding as he looks around*] Still pretty shithouse.

RON: Not for long.

DEN: [*finally*] Am I supposed to – what's going on?

RON: Eh? What do you mean – Jeannie wrote and told you surely.

DEN: No.

RON: You're joking.

> [*As he fishes through his wallet for a card.*]

Hasn't changed, your sister. Still only does exactly what suits her.

> [*He finds a card and gives it to* DEN.]

They put our photos in the union newsletter –

DEN: Swap you for a Vita-Brit card.

RON: And you're all meant to have been briefed.

DEN: I more or less keep my head down.

> [DEN *is unsure as to whether he should keep the card or not.*]

RON: Keep it, where we're staying's on the back. The firm scores their first government contract and it's here. Like the old days, you'll be able to keep your eye on me.

DEN: You're with the outfit doing this review.

RON: [*correcting him*] Intervention. Intervention. Which is to say
the place has been fucked over – as you know – and we're
going to turn it around. [*Quickly looking around at the
works*] If I'd ever taken acid I'd think I was having a
flashback. Someone's painted the canteen, that much I did
notice.

DEN: Put a roof on it, I think.

RON: [*enjoying himself*] I keep thinking I'll come face to face
with myself coming around a corner. A twenty-year-old
hoon. And look at you. This is going to be good. I'll be flat
out but it's going to be good.

  [*He picks up the scattered transparencies, wiping them.*]

DEN: They brought you all the way over.

RON: We're the best. Couldn't get out of Perth quick enough.
Cowboys and wankers, don't bother going there.

DEN: I probably wouldn't.

RON: Eh – the Northern beaches has come along.

DEN: Jeannie's style up there now.

RON: I don't know, she's right at home in Perth. I would've
written to you myself...

  [*DEN looks back at the card.*]

DEN: We had these other consultants just before the cutbacks.

RON: Completely different. We're good. We also charge through
the nose so they don't call us in unless they want action.

DEN: Their report said we should be more enthusiastic. And
before that a task force

RON: Lots of task and not much force.

  [*Pause*]

DEN: You've done well. Always wear a suit?

RON: First day. Well, I'll be relying on you mate, steer me in
the right direction.

DEN: I wouldn't know too much.

RON: You will. Can't have too much info and we're going to
analyse the shit out of this place.

DEN: You'd want to be talking to someone else.

RON: Well, I have just been quoting you to our client, the Minister, just the other day.

DEN: Me?

RON: 'My brother-in-law's in your Engineering Works, he'll tell you how many contracts have been lost over the last ten years, many of which have gone offshore.'

DEN: I hope he doesn't ring me up.

RON: He gets this hot flush that starts over his collar and spreads, the Minister. Very slowly, it's marvellous to watch. I said, 'All right, four years ago you upgraded the foundry, but where's the investment for the rest of the plant?' Flush. 'You've got one of the country's most highly skilled work forces' . . . and then I got him – 'So start winning back contracts.' Flush, flush. 'And stop whingeing about profits' flush, flush – 'Because the Engineering Works is a public asset and because your brief's to make water pipes and bridges and bits of gaols that no-one else'd want to touch.' Flush, flush, flush. [*Smiling*] Want me to do it again?

DEN: You kept quiet about the screwdrivers?

RON: I'm a junkie for all this. Still a hoon. I mean, is that it or is that it?

DEN: You enjoy it, that's the main thing.

RON: Happy as a fish out of wa – pig in shit, whatever it is.

DEN: Well, good luck, but if the pope walked in here I don't know that anyone'd believe him.

RON: Tomorrow night's news, and that's between us. Watch it.

DEN: You're full of energy, I'll give you that, but I reckon you might be a bit late.

RON: Now, you were never a live wire mate but you used to have a bit more spark.

[*Pause*]

DEN: I came here for a temporary job twenty-five years ago.

RON: We both did.

[*Pause.* RON *is setting up to keep moving his stuff.*]

I have to ask about the trains, the kids still talk about them.

DEN: Packed away mostly. All the points got pretty cranky.

RON: And the birds.

DEN: Not since we lost that bit of bush up the back. And the ones in the aviary died. About a week before the old man.

> [*Silence.* RON *collects his things.*]

RON: Well, I was going to ask about your love life, but I don't know if I'm game. Hopefully you've got someone who can use my standard gift from Singapore.

> [*He throws* DEN *a plastic shopping bag from Singapore, and starts wheeling off.*]

And if you're still a vestal virgin you can always wear it yourself.

> [RON *goes. There are sounds of various radio stations [one classical, one Macedonian]. A toilet flushes.* DEN *takes the wrapped present from the bag, and puts it in his work bag [an old-fashioned airways bag].*]

BARBARA *in her room at the boarding house. Clothes are scattered on the floor, which she tidies up as* DEN *arrives. He has arrived unannounced, which has put* BARBARA *into a panic.*

BARBARA: It's not that I mind. It's just on the door. Guests of the opposite sex. I mean this isn't me. I am accustomed to a bit more space. Like an entire house.

DEN: Well, she let me in.

BARBARA: She'd be on the turps, that's why. [*Sniffing*] Oh, smell that, why anyone'd cook a chop at this hour. . . Next it'll be the black pudding down the hall and we'll all be keeling over backwards.

> [*She looks at* DEN, *having attempted to pick up a few pieces of underwear.*]

Not much point in tidying up. It'd all still look the same. Everything you've got in the one room.

DEN: I rattle about in my old place.

BARBARA: Even makes the nice things look like shit. I said to Barry, 'Have the lot, have everything', and he said, 'Good. Thanks very much I will'.

[*He has a newspaper in his workbag.*]

DEN: I don't know if you saw this. Last night on the telly. [*He looks around.*] Then I remembered you said you didn't have one. [*She goes to take the paper.*] Not too close, I pong a bit. [*He reads the paper.*] The brother-in-law tipped me off and I didn't believe it. Braddon was on last night. The Minister. Guarantees our jobs for at least ten years. At least. I think he said it twice. We can feel free to take out a mortgage, buy that car, pay off the second boat. And the big sort of review they're doing. Well. It's something. Things might shift. He sounded pretty convincing. I mean – I could take you out for a feed tonight and still come out on top. [*He realises what he has said.*] Oh, that's terrible. I didn't mean that. Not that way. Oh, god.

[*Pause. She hands him back the paper.*]

BARBARA: Good.

[*Pause*]

DEN: Of course you've got a lot of go in you. Something you have to remember.

[*He fumbles in his bag for the present, unsure as to whether it is an appropriate time to give it.*]

BARBARA: Oh have I? Oh, is that what I've got? You'll laugh at this then. Barbara big mouth. I got a job all right. In at Diamond's this time, sewing up little baby's dingo suits. First bell at 8.14, last bell at 4.14. No going to the toilet an hour after morning tea or an hour after lunch. Whole fucking kit and caboodle. Now you know. And there I am. Brand new life.

DEN: You shouldn't have to work there. Not you.

BARBARA: Eighty-four women there. Why would I think I'm any different.

DEN: Wouldn't be too many around like you. At least you haven't given up.

[*Pause. She lights a cigarette. He has the parcel out of the bag, and gives it to her. She takes it, it has been a*

*long time since someone has given her a present. She
does not open it.*]
BARBARA: You think I didn't think about you, but I did. You've
got something in you. You know what I mean. Something
there. Something nice. Then I think, no. Too quiet for me.
He's too quiet for me. I told you all that, anyway.
DEN: We didn't even give it a real go. We should have.
[*She starts to unwrap it.*]
BARBARA: [*trying to explain*] See, you don't sort of need so
much.
DEN: I always thought I was sort of missing my life. Other
people –
BARBARA: Oh other people. Other people are just acting.
[BARBARA *slides the happy coat from its wrappings. She
looks at* DEN.]
DEN: I just wanted you to have it. No strings attached.
[*She pushes it back into the wrappings, keeps it, and
starts to move him towards the door.*]
BARBARA: Sorry. Not my fault. It's on the back of the door.
Thanks for this, I'm sure it'll be lovely. [*Watching him go*]
It's all a race, you'd never keep up with me.
[BARBARA *watches* DEN *leave then bundles up her parcel
and goes. The sounds of the boarding house blend into
silence.*]

*A girl walks along with a suitcase, looks at her bus-pass and
leaves.*

*In the sunlight outside the fabrication shop at the State
Engineering Works,* DEN *looks at his watch, puts down his
cowboy novel, takes his crib box from his airways bag – it's
time to eat another sandwich. It has been in the sun, however,
and the tomato is very soggy. He peels it open, balances the
bread and proceeds to peel it off. A soccer ball flies towards*

him and he rolls it back. He would just like to be left alone.
RON *approaches.*

RON: Right. I wondered where you got to.

    [RON *starts to sit.*]

DEN: They're good slacks. I wouldn't sit there – not in those good slacks.

RON: Haven't you ever heard of washable Guccis? [*Sitting*] Incredible view, look at that. You could be anywhere. That could be the Mediterranean.

    [*Pause*]

Well, I think so far so good. The doors back on the toilets is a start. A small step for industrial democracy but all part of the New Workplace capital 'N' capital 'W'. And as for clocking on for all or none, I think it'll be none from the look on management's faces.

DEN: I didn't really see them. . .

RON: All trying to look keen, because they know – first step we shaft the rats. The big black taxi for about a third of upstairs. Should please you blokes.

    [*Very little response from* DEN. *He is still fiddling with his sandwich.*]

DEN: Left these too long. Sun's made the tomatoes soggy.

RON: Still pommy army philosophy, eh? If they're no good at what they do, promote them.

DEN: It's devon if you're hungry.

RON: No, I'm right, I'm due for a conference in a tick.

DEN: Family tradition. Betty reckoned the old man couldn't tell the difference between this and ham – so that's what he got for forty-five years.

RON: That meeting in there just now –

DEN: Fridays she used to make him pick the devon off.

RON: I talked to you just now in that meeting, you barely answered. Look, I know what it's like – you've been told you don't know shit, and suddenly I'm telling you you do. But this is me.

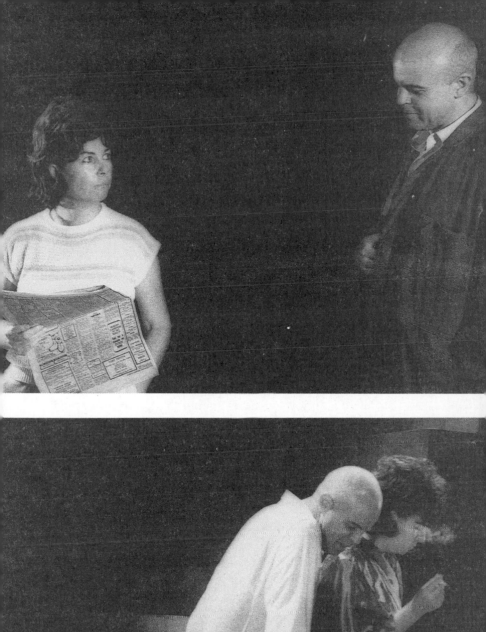

[DEN *is examining the devon, there may still be a rim of plastic to be peeled off.*]

DEN: [*the devon*] I don't know that I've ever really looked at it. Closely. Peculiar flecks of colour when you think about it.

RON: I mean, you didn't have to stay being a labourer, a T.A. You speak English for one thing.

DEN: Anything could be squashed in there, who'd know.

RON: Look, I'm sure it's riveting but have you finished?

[DEN *puts the sandwich back in the box. The ball comes back in.* RON *makes sure that he is the one who sends it back.*]

DEN: Heroes in their own lunchtime, those two blokes.

RON: All right – you probably never thought you'd still be here. But you are. And I haven't forgotten that you're the one who pushed me out of that gate, shoved my first year uni fees in my hand –

DEN: You paid me back. That's the past.

RON: But there's no joy for me in seeing this place turn round if you end up dead in the water.

DEN: [*with difficulty*] Look, no offence mate, but when that siren goes I'm the one has to go back in there. And we'll have another go at pressing these new back gates for the hoppers. It's the third time they've been sent back. They don't sit flush and we just keep working and reworking them –

RON: And sending them down the line. . .

DEN: I'm not saying I'm. . . [*Smart*]. . . but they weren't in spec when we did them the first time.

RON: Prisoners of process we call it.

DEN: Do you.

RON: And we've all seen the final product. Lumps of coal trickling onto the tracks. Impresses your customers no end. I'm telling you we can turn all that around. We're commissioned to.

DEN: Well, good luck to you, I'm just grateful to be working.

RON: You're going into one of my groups. Stage one for the moment. They're voluntary and you're in one. To start putting you blokes in control.

DEN: I just let my mind go blank.

RON: Well, don't worry it's only brainwashing. Basically you'll enjoy it. Working in with the good guys from management – your old man'd turn in his grave.

DEN: You paid me back. I never even think about it.

[*As* RON *reaches for* DEN'*s book*]

RON: [*reading*] 'Fleeing Arizona'. . . [*He looks at* DEN.] 'Texan Ted makes his way to California'. . .

[*The siren sounds.* DEN *looks at his watch and slowly collects his things.*]

Before you go, something you might like to know. That task force did a skills audit. You scored a mention.

DEN: Me? No.

RON: Fifty-year-old labourer X, untrained, whose skill on the drilling machine is such that should he be off sick they hold off any drilling work until he gets back.

DEN: Just cheaper to use me rather than a tradesman.

RON: Nothing personal, mate but your self-esteem's halfway down Death Valley at the moment. If you could jack it up it'd be a help.

[*He gives him back the book.*]

'Texan Ted'. . .

DEN: Never fails to win. And he always gets the girl on the last page.

[*The hooter sounds fully.* DEN *puts the book in his pocket and goes, then turns and watches* RON *walking away in the opposite direction. We hear the sound of a distant tuba.*]

DEN'*s house. The tuba stops.* BARBARA *is swishing in her happy coat. They have just made love,* DEN'*s self-esteem has indeed risen a notch.* BARBARA *laughs.* DEN *is getting dressed. An occasional coal truck rumbles by.*

BARBARA: [*the joke*] What?

> [BARBARA *shakes her head. She lights a cigarette. And laughs again.*]

No offence but, I'd never have picked you. . .

DEN: What?

BARBARA: [*laughing*] You really are a very good driller. Honest.

DEN: Oh well. . . if you think about something long enough.

> [*Pause*]

You look nice. Sitting there.

> [BARBARA *leans back, relishing her cigarette and her happy coat. She momentarily ponders the relationship.*]

BARBARA: Oh, why not for heaven's sake. Why not? It just hit me – why not? Why not?

DEN: That's more or less what I kept saying.

BARBARA: You fight romance and it'll blow up in your face – I've still got my goals, you can't expect another person to be everything, how can they?

DEN: So we'll give it a go.

BARBARA: We said! At least I made you fight for me, that's something. Anyway I'd never've got this. [*The happy coat. Pause*] Still, one step at a time.

DEN: What I think is people need to stop being scared of each other. My father – he used to come home from that mine, and after every shift, as his hand touched the flyscreen door we'd hear. 'You know what those bastards did today?'

BARBARA: [*fiddling with some embroidery on her coat*] Exhausting.

DEN: Too right.

BARBARA: Den, you know that time I went in the country and western night –

DEN: Yes –

BARBARA: Did I make a fool of myself, you know, singing –

DEN: *Suspicious Minds*? No.

BARBARA:. . . Did I look scared?

DEN: Only when the cigarette fell out of your mouth and dropped in your guitar.

BARBARA: [*laughing*] Shut up. What guitar. Was I the worst one there?

DEN: No. There was worse than you. You were really very brave.

[*Pause*]

I did try that public speaking business. . . mostly estate agents and bank clerks. . .

BARBARA: Oh, you don't take any notice of them. Now or never. That's what I reckon.

Sound of BARBARA's *a capella rendering of* Suspicious Minds, *as* DEN *goes from the boarding house to the W.E.A public speaking class.* DEN *sits. As soon as he sits he gets up quickly, and picks a folded piece of paper out of a bucket. He makes an awkward little joke about not looking at it and sits again. Suddenly he is called on to go first. He rises quickly, panicked.* BARBARA's *singing stops.*

DEN: Right. . . Well. I'm back. I've missed a few so you'll have to. . . Won't take long. As you can probably remember. . .

[*He considers asking whether he could go later, then decides against it. He prepares himself for public speaking – stands on two feet, hands out of pockets, puts them in again. He loses his topic in one of the pockets and has to fossick for it. His palms sweat etc. This is his version of hell.*]

Oh, hell. [*Finds the paper. Smiles*] Two minutes up yet? Just joking. What topic did I have to speak on last time. . . 'Shirts'. Ah well, let's have a look. Or will I put everyone out of their misery and give up now. . . [*As he unwraps the piece of paper, he becomes even more nervous.*]

Here goes. Right. [*Somewhat relieved*] Trains. Well, there you go. Well, they're very good. Trains. Rolling stock.

[*Pause*]

Perhaps I should go back to the shirts. . . You don't get tired
of looking at them when they're well-built. The welds.
Occasional wooden finish. We build them, of course. When
I say we, I – the State Engineering Works. Of course you
wouldn't take a ride in what we build. Coal wagons, bulk
hoppers. [*Floundering*] And they're not so interesting. [*He
re-examines the slip of paper.*] Train. . . journeys. People
have their favourites. Some are well-known. I haven't done
any. [*Remembering*] But my grandfather did leave me four
one-pound notes to take a trip, across the west coast of
Scotland right to the ferry for the Isle of Skye. If I ever got
there. Which I haven't. The Kyle Line. [*He is surprised by
the memory.*] Best to sit on the right hand side. And there
isn't a refreshment carriage. [*Pause. He has run out of things
to say.*] He'd tell me about these curlews. No nest, curlews.
Lay their eggs on the bare ground.
    'Where the old plain men have rosy faces
    and the young fair maidens quiet eyes'.
This grandfather, used to memorise a couple of stanzas every
morning while he shaved.
    [*Pause. The bell sounds. His time is up. This is the first
    time* DEN *has spoken to the bell.* DEN *cannot believe it. He
    wipes his sweaty palms with a handkerchief, looks at his
    watch, and returns to his seat. He turns back to the
    'group', fairly pleased with himself.*]
Sorry, I thought of something else. While I've got a run up.
To give you an idea about people and trains. The
grandfather'd do the trip once a year, and always sat with a
compass and a notebook, taking notes. So that he always
knew, at any given moment, precisely what direction the
train was going in. [*Returns to seat*] Which gives you an
idea of how people are when it comes to trains.
    [DEN *sits. As far as he is concerned he will probably
    never get up and talk again, but he has given it his best
    shot.*]

BARBARA *runs into* DEN, *who is still sitting in the chair. He reaches out to kiss her, she throws him a pair of runners.*

BARBARA: Come on! Now! Oh god, this is it, this is it, this is it. The thing is of course Den, that not even when I'm bored shitless do I let my mind go numb. That's my secret. Sometimes I get so many ideas I think they must belong to someone else.

[*This transformation keeps* DEN *in his seat.*]

You're being dull. Already.

DEN: Deep down you think I'm dull. We'll never last.

BARBARA: We will. We said.

[*She disappears to walk around the rocks as* DEN *puts on his shoes.* RON *appears, dressing to go into the works – taking off his jacket, putting on a hard hat.* DEN *remains where he is and listens to* RON.]

RON: The big picture is, and it's why we're moving so fast, and this is keep it to yourself – China's on the lookout for passenger trains. No private firms can come close to this capacity. All we have to do is get processes running uphill again.

[*Pause*]

There's a lot of work in a passenger train. And when they start drawing up retraining lists your name should be at the top. Pick up a career path and move along the ladder. Your welder's ticket, electronics. . . it'd be a good idea to make the right decision.

[BARBARA *reappears.*]

BARBARA: Come on.

[RON *disappears and* DEN *now follows* BARBARA.]

I only want to go as far as the point.

DEN: Which is only as far as you can go. . .

BARBARA: There. There it is.

[DEN *looks.*]

And the thing is, I'm not too late. It hasn't even been finished yet. You tell me what you see.

DEN: City Beach. The boat harbour here. The old fish and chip shop that burnt down. [*Looks back to the beach*] That great thing going up at the rate of knots.

BARBARA: Resort Beach International Resort.

DEN: I don't know why they're calling it that. People'll get confused. It's City Beach.

BARBARA: They're changing the name of the beach, to fit the hotel. Why not, they've got the money. Why shouldn't they? 'City Beach'. City Beach. It doesn't make sense anyway. Listen to this, see all those windows, not one single one of those windows has any kind of view of the steelworks. Or the State Engineering Works. Or anything revolting. Design. 'What industry?', you'd say up there. 'I can't see anything. Whack some more champagne in the orange juice'. All the beach and up the back of the escarpment. I mean that's more or less rainforest that escarpment. Rainforest! Rainforest's fashionable, always going on about it. It's a goldmine and why not? Why shouldn't we have a goldmine here? Japs see all that sand, they won't be able to stop themselves. Yanks'll be flying here direct.

DEN: I don't know that people'd come down here for a holiday.

BARBARA: We think we don't deserve this, that's the problem. The entire city's got an inferiority complex. You know what international means? They know how to make a go of it and they know what the fuck they're doing. A lovely pink palace.

DEN: Bit of work for tradesmen on it. . .

BARBARA: And think how many people they're gonna need to run it. They'll have to take some locals, Den. The Labour Council'll make them take some locals. But what calibre of person are they going to get? They won't be wanting Miss Macedonia from Kentucky Fried or Doris from Dapto who lost her finger in the tin plate mill. I don't want to be mean but they'll be after a different class of person. And when those cranes come off that roof and they put a bathplug in every room and wrap all those toilets in all that white ribbon like they do – who do you reckon's going to be there? Part of the team. They're having teams. I'm not going to be distracted from this, Den.

DEN: I see.

BARBARA: I'm not stupid. I've gone into it. I know my age. You don't go for waitressing or behind the bar, women my age are hostesses. Here's your table, where's your waiter, here's the conference room. Have a nice conference. I know I'm rough around the edges, I'm not stupid, you might think I am.

DEN: I don't.

BARBARA: I know you have to look the part. Like you were eating croysants before anyone else had heard of them. [*She presents him with some brochures.*] You can do anything these days. Well you have to. Now this course, or – [*She takes a quick look at the brochures.*] I suppose you'd say diploma – it's not only for models. Or teenagers. Personally tailored to fit your requirements. It's not one of those crummy ones. It's a proper Academy.

[*Pause*]

A brand new start.

DEN: [*reads slowly*] Strike, it's expensive.

BARBARA: Only if you did the lot. Which you would do. You've got your grooming, there's a lot in that. Your deportment. Your social skills and communication. Your elocution. Your colours done, that's the first thing. Where are you if you don't know your colours. Exceptional extras.

DEN: Optional extras.

BARBARA: It's not modelling. I'm not stupid.

DEN: [*looking at* BARBARA] No. No. I see that. It's just – expensive.

BARBARA: It's. . . intensive. You won't know me.

[*Pause*]

I haven't got the money.

[DEN *looks up at her.*]

Well you knew that. I've never made a secret of that. I had bloody Barry, frittering it away. Never have a joint cheque account. And I was never bonus-hungry, just run up my quota. Why go over, it's exactly what they want.

[*Pause*]

It's practically full-time.

DEN: The sheilas who are running it. . .

BARBARA: Look like a million bucks. I've checked them out.

[*Pause*]

I've got an artist's impression of that hotel on my fridge. You know what I mean?

[BARBARA *is starting to realise that he may not pay.*]

DEN: It's just very expensive.

BARBARA: I wouldn't ask you but it's an investment.

DEN: How do you know you'd like it?

BARBARA: I just knew something was going to hit me.

DEN: It's not so much the money.

BARBARA: It is a lot of money.

DEN: I'm just a bit conservative, I realise that. . . [*He looks to the hotel*] Still, it'd be a job you could always go back to.

[BARBARA *is unsure as to what he means.*]

What I was saying before. A baby. . . You wouldn't be too old. . .

BARBARA: [*eyes on the hotel, hiding her disappointment*] Oh, twice as old as me, you see it in the papers all the time. [*Distracted*] The Andes or somewhere. . .

[*Sound of a band in the distance. Playing the same song that the tuba was practising earlier.*]

DEN: Miners' Federation Band. The old man used to play in it.

BARBARA: I always like to cry whenever I see a brass band.

[*Nearly in tears, she starts to take the brochures out of* DEN's *hands.*]

DEN: I'll hang on to these.

BARBARA: [*excited*] Not them lot. That lot's so old, every time they go out marching someone else drops dead. They've hardly got any instruments left, it's all done with tape-recorders. [*To* DEN] Definitely no tuba. [*The brochures*] Have a look? Think about it, eh?

[*Pause*]
Everywhere I've ever worked, they check your bag when you
leave for the day. They wouldn't do that there.
[*She has been smoking a cigarette. As she turns she looks
up at the hotel. She decides to give up smoking.*]
[*excited that* DEN *has not said 'no' and stamping out her
cigarette.*] Right, that's the last one. Dead give-away, aren't
they? Common. Lucky thing I never had my ears pierced.
[*The band continues to play in the distance.*]

DEN *and* BARBARA *move off in different directions.* BARBARA
watches the band and just as she is about to follow them MARJ,
her sister, enters. She only has to look sideways at BARBARA
and BARBARA *is deflated.* MARJ *carries a highly embroidered
priest's chasuble which she is in the process of repairing. She
gestures with a pair of scissors.*

MARJ: I only want to know if you need some help. I am your
sister – why won't you return my calls? If you need help,
you know I'm prepared to come down. I don't mind how
many times I have to keep doing it, I'm only too happy to
come down and help you. Provided we can discuss Virginia.
Who is, we mustn't forget, a little like me. She's a lot like
me, she needs a sense of continuity. I can imagine how
you're feeling – if I was ever to marry, which I don't
suppose I will, I'd be very upset if it didn't last. [*Too*] Please
remember though that the three of us can constitute a family,
Barbara. Yes, it might be very sad, but we can.
[BARBARA *looks at her with contempt and follows the
band.*]

DEN'S *place.* DEN *and* RON *are at the model railway. They are
watching a locomotive and carriages lurch along a track.* DEN
is pleased – it is the first time in years that he has used it. RON

and DEN *spend the scene willing the thing to run smoothly.* DEN
occasionally dusts things off.

DEN: [*laughing*] I wouldn't be any good. You reckon I'd be any
good? As long as it's not some sort of favour.
   [*He fiddles with a point.*]

RON: Your temperament test said detail-minded. Very useful you
detail-mindeds. Not much good on your own, but put you in
together – [*To the train*] you-think-you-can-you-think-you-
can. . . whoo-ooo . . .

DEN: [*looking askance at* RON] But statistics? Statistics? A
shovel donkey like me.

RON: We've trained hundreds of people thicker than you. And
look at this – hand-built under-carriages
   [*He bumps a bit of the set as he tries to pick up a train.*]
  Oh, sorry –

DEN: It'd take me more than five days, I'd have to do it twice -

RON: [*ignoring his self-deprecation*] And ongoing training a day
or so a month – there'll be dozens of teams all through the
plant collecting data instead of having a whinge.

DEN: All right, take those hopper gates. They rattle. They're in
spec but they rattle. I don't see that. . .

RON: You'll have charts and graphs to sort it out, where it's
going wrong. Statistical process control.

DEN: I like the old way. I tell someone it's not flush and they
tell me to fuck off.

RON: And if quality continues to be poor, you'll be expected to
stop the line. [*The train*] Yes! yes! Ding, ding, ding.

DEN: You don't reckon you're not still a bit of a two bob lair.

RON: Mate, the last place we worked with went from nearly
closing to number two nationally and could be about to start
taking on apprentices again. The Japs have been teaching
their blokes for years.

DEN: All right, I'll be in on it.

RON: Good on you – you won't know yourself – you'll –
   [*As* RON *stands or shifts his legs he completely squashes
a small cottage.*]

Sorry mate, I think I just demolished the Presbyterian Church.

DEN: Community service probably. . . I'm just amazed it hasn't all seized up.

[*Pause.* RON *gets a fax out of his pocket.*]

RON: Almost forgot, had a fax from home, from Jeannie.

DEN: A fax at home – you deserve each other, you two.

RON: She's on again about selling this place. Don't blame me, blame your mother for leaving it to her. Only because she's got the shits with me, 'I do have my own investments', and so on. She'll change her mind.

[DEN *remains quiet.*]

Wouldn't hurt to give her a ring.

DEN: I know practically every mark on every wall.

RON: Do you good to have a place of your own, a bachelor unit down on the beach. . . Or set yourself up with a wealthy woman. They always fall for blokes like you.

[RON *leaves.* DEN *moves away as* BARBARA *appears. She is paying a lot more attention to her grooming, and wears a slip and a pair of high heels which she is breaking in.*]

BARBARA: You can't expect me to see you every day, Den. You have no idea of what goes through me at the Academy – Poise-this. Poise-that. I'm not having a lot of success with poise, and frankly, at the moment, it's all that concerns me.

[*She slips a dress over her head and joins* MARJ.]

The sound of a leagues club in the daytime. MARJ *is standing in a queue, and* BARBARA *joins her.* BARBARA *is mortified because they are wearing identical dresses,* BARBARA'S *is obviously a copy – cheaper fabric, cut, etc. They are a very prominent colour. A number is called. It is not theirs.* MARJ'S *calmness and reasonableness only serve to increase* BARBARA'S *sullenness.*

MARJ: [*looking around*] I don't know that we'll ever get a table . . . [*The dress*] Oh, never mind. You just forgot that I had this frock. No-one's to blame.

[*A number is called out and* BARBARA *looks at a ticket.*]
But I was wearing it at Christmas. Last Christmas. Barry
even commented. You've forgotten. I think you said how
nice I looked. I'm sure you said that. So when you saw it in
. . . wherever, you went ahead and bought it. Just forgot.
And it's quite a good copy.

[*Silence from* BARBARA]
Might as well give it to you now. No point waiting till we sit
down.

[*She fishes in her bag for* BARBARA*'s present.*]
BARBARA: Hopefully it's a bucket of dye.

[*She hands* BARBARA *an envelope.*]
MARJ: Just a cheque, I thought that was best. Happy Birthday.
And a card from Virginia.

[BARBARA *puts it straight into her bag without opening
it.*]
BARBARA: Thank you.
MARJ: You should have let me take you to a proper restaurant.
I would have booked. I wouldn't have minded. I don't worry
about the price of an STD call. It would have been a treat for
me, I don't eat out very much. It wouldn't have been any
trouble. Going to a proper restaurant where we could have
booked.

[*Pause*]
No-one's been talking about you. Matron simply suggested
that what she would like is a letter from you. It's not
unreasonable. You could write her a letter, Barbara. That
Virginia is to come to me each weekend. They'll be talking
community housing soon – well it would be nice if she was
prepared. It might seem strange to you, Barbara but she's
company for me. I have put some effort into her, Barbara.
Not that I've thought of it as effort. Not that it's effort when
it's your only niece.
BARBARA: It is a restaurant, Marj. We are in a restaurant.
MARJ: Barbara, it's a leagues club. Look – it says so on the
carpet.

BARBARA: Marj, it's a proper restaurant. In a club. It's new. They've got to put restaurants somewhere. You might like to think we're a lot of peasants, but. . . There's a real demand these days. For restaurants. Marj.

[*Silence*]

MARJ: I've got her wearing deodorant, Barbara. And shaving. They didn't seem to be insisting on that. I have her getting the train into Central every Friday afternoon, changing once and then taking the ferry to my place. No panic whatsoever. She actually likes going to the symphony. And she waits now until everyone else starts clapping. But I do, as I said, need to know. It can't just be one in five, whenever the mood takes her. Not really. Now you're single, you'll see. Weekends can be very difficult.

[MARJ *picks what she thinks is a hair from* BARBARA'*s dress.*]

Oh, I beg your pardon, it's a thread. There's not the finish on garments these days.

[BARBARA *seethes. A number is called.* MARJ *tries to see their number but* BARBARA *keeps it to herself. Her high heels are killing her.*]

We're lucky one of us has a home she can come to. As matron said, and there was no criticism intended, if her mother can only visit birthdays and Christmas. . .

BARBARA: I send money. I've never missed a week.

MARJ: No-one's saying you don't contribute.

[*Pause*]

If you're thinking I should have her through the week, I can't. Not at the moment. . . There's nothing for her there, at the presbytery.

BARBARA: Don't tell me you're still going there, Marj. Can't a pack of priests manage to look after themselves?

MARJ: [*laughing*] Hardly. Hardly. Oh, I could imagine that. Outsiders can't imagine the work involved. Never mind their meals, and trips to the podiatrist – I'm run off my feet with basic vestment repair. Still. . . I enjoy it. . .

[BARBARA *peers into the restaurant. The high heels are killing her.*]

BARBARA: You would really wonder why people can't just eat and get it over with.

MARJ: Matron can't really tell her what to do, she'd rather have the note from you.

[*Another number is called. This time it is theirs but* BARBARA *doesn't even listen.*]

Perhaps we could eat in there? Pie with gravy and a milk shake? [*Comfort food*]

BARBARA: I'm not having my birthday in a snack bar. I'd never even go in there. It's a snack bar. Why would you think I'd ever go in there?

MARJ: I'm happy to wait. [*Looking at the two dresses*] Very funny. Really. Like we're in uniform.

BARBARA: [*glaring*] Don't you think I look a bit different? Different style?

MARJ: Yes I do. This is not a colour I'd ever pick for you.

BARBARA: It's a colour I'm meant to wear a lot.

[*The same number is called out again.* BARBARA *still does not register.*]

MARJ: I wouldn't have thought so.

BARBARA: I mean, I have been told. And I know myself, I know what colours I'm meant to wear. Exactly in fact.

MARJ: [*the dress*] And it's a very good copy.

BARBARA: And this colour's one of them.

MARJ: It is a very good copy. You wonder why you bother spending money on the real thing.

BARBARA: I don't know if you know what you're talking about. One thing that I do happen to know about is how clothes are made. They're all copies, that's how clothes are made. Someone does a sleeve, someone does a zip and some fat tart climbs into them.

[*The number's called again, and is ignored.*]

I don't know what you're talking about.

MARJ: It's just that I know what this cost. Mind you, I'll have it for years.

BARBARA: I'd have no idea what this cost. The fella who buys my clothes won't let me look at the price tag.

MARJ: What fellow? Who? What are you talking about.

[BARBARA *smiles.*]

You're not. . . you're not somebody's mistress. Oh, Barbara, you don't.

BARBARA: Don't be bloody ridiculous. I do it for nothing. Same as you. Slip 'em one on the side. Presbytery curtains drawn to keep out the afternoon sun.

MARJ: They are priests! Oh my godfather, Barbara. I think you're mad, that's all there is to it –

[*They manage to remember that they are in a public place.*]

BARBARA: Oh well, you're nuts, so we're even.

MARJ: I know what all this is, don't think I don't. I got mummy's earrings. Well, take the flaming things if it'd make you a nicer person.

BARBARA: Leave Verge alone.

[BARBARA *pushes the number into* MARJ's *hand. But* MARJ *grabs* BARBARA's *arm before she moves away. While this is going on* DEN *and* RON *enter the factory floor. In the shadow we see* RON *climbing up to take down a noose.*]

MARJ: I got the taxi to drive past that boarding house you're staying in, don't tell me you don't need help. Mummy said it. Daddy said it. You're nothing but a drifter. And you know very well what happens to drifters, Barbara.

[BARBARA *pries herself away and leaves.* MARJ *tries to think what does happen to drifters.*]

Well, it isn't very pleasant.

[MARJ *realises that people have noticed them, and she searches for the exit.*]

VERGE *[Virginia] enters and looks towards where* MARJ *and* BARBARA *have been. She wheels her suitcases in a shopping trolley.*

VERGE: I've got this story about them, this story about my mother. But what you want to know is, who won. It's a true story because it's forbidden to talk about it. It's forbidden to talk to the driver while the bus is in motion. Last Christmas. How dare, how dare, how dare you bring that up. But which one do you dare go swimming with. Which one. Two sisters in a lake, near an ocean which was yellow, not the ocean but the lake. And parents on the sand who should have been watching it's obvious. Two little sisters who couldn't swim, and one walks out a bit too far. Then she reaches and grabs the cossie of the other one and pulls her out further and below, under the yellow water, and struggles up on her shoulders like water-ski wonderland on the telly.

[*She looks to where the two women were, imitating.*]

'It was your fault, you climbed on me.' 'Don't be ridiculous, Barbara, you pulled me out. You were the one. You climbed on me.' So if your number came up, which one would you rather be in the water with. . . which one. . . .

[*She leaves.*]

The fabrication shop floor. Just out of RON's *reach is a noose. Furious, he is trying to pull it down.* DEN *approaches, walking from the back of a group that has just dispersed. He has welding cable over his shoulder, a clipboard and a ladder. There is the sound of work around them, slowly starting up again. Intermittently, there is also the tuba.*

DEN: That was a bit rough – you don't want to – [. . . *Take it personally*]

RON: It's out and out industrial bastardry. One thing pushes me to the wall, it's conspiracy theories. Jesus.

DEN: Oh well, ex-miners, they get a bit irritable.

RON: You don't think you're being a bit harsh?

DEN: [*the noose*] I'll do that.

RON: Belligerent arseholes I would have said. I thought the cutbacks cleared out the trouble-makers. If any more get shed they're first on my list.

DEN: Nothing personal – people worry they'll have to skill down – or losing conditions –

RON: I'm talking about empowering people, breaking down fucking hierarchies. Making the place more efficient. If I just announced we were going to start ripping off their balls, I don't remember saying it.

DEN: No you were clear. Terrific the way you explained things. And those cause-effect diagram sessions are really going well.

[RON *is distracted. Looking at a group of men in the distance.*]

RON: Nothing bodgie about what we teach, mate.

DEN: We've been applying it to welding rods, there's been a hold-up with them for years – the upshot of it was we're going to by-pass supply and start ordering them ourselves. [*Smiling*] Spent half my life apologising to welders.

RON: Well, they're all having a dekko at you – consorting with the enemy. [*Through clenched teeth*] Consultants not executioners, darling.

DEN: You're doing a good job.

RON: Well thanks for speaking up for me, thanks for the support.

DEN: Oh.

RON: You could have said a few words, mate. Everybody else was.

DEN: Fair enough.

RON: Spread this around if you like – personnel's asked for a list. Who'd be suitable for retraining. It's very early, possibly a directive from the Minister.

DEN: Reserving places in college?

RON: It's one thing to persuade your appalling, grossly confident management that some changes might be necessary, you'd think it'd be obvious to these jokers.

[*As* RON *goes*]

DEN: See all this multi-skilling, some of them find it a bit confusing. . .

RON: And do me a favour and give Jeannie a ring. She's the last person I need on my back.

[*Sound of the tuba*]

BARBARA *is moving into* DEN's. *Lighting suggests the various rooms in which one or two items have been present throughout the play. The tuba, model railway etc.* BARBARA *has been out in the back yard, and enters. She wears very high heels, and the deportment classes are having their effect. She is clearly imitating her teachers but the effect is less than stylish. She is aware of her every gesture and has one or two favourites which she is currently working up.* BARBARA *has a glass of champagne in her hand, which* DEN *refills from time to time. He doesn't drink.* DEN *has just carried in the last of her 'luggage' – a garbage bag and a beauty case.*

BARBARA: You did that for me! You built that entire fucking –

[*She stops dead.*]

See that's the thing. What do you say instead of fucking?

[*Pause*]

You built that fence for me.

DEN: No.

BARBARA: You did.

DEN: As soon as you said yes, I knocked it into shape. It's a bit jerry. . . not much time. . . you want everything to be right.

BARBARA: Here I am! A brand new start! It was the black pudding finally made up my mind, of course.

[DEN *has flowers for her.*]

Roses!

DEN: Silk. I thought, well, that way you've got them.

BARBARA: [*she improves her vowel*] Roses!

[*She glides out to have another look at the fence.*]
Oh, and it works. I defy anyone to see any part of that steelworks from any part of that backyard. You could put a pool in there.
[*She returns.*]

DEN: . . . If we could dig through the rock

BARBARA: Now, I don't wantcha – want you – to think I'm taking – all this for granted.

DEN: [*the champagne*] I hope I got the right sort. I –
[BARBARA *walks towards him, takes a big sip of champagne, kisses him and squirts some into his mouth. A coal truck goes past.*]
Well. A first time for everything. Oh. I thought it'd be a bit more bitter. Champagne.

BARBARA: But can I really change whatever I want?

DEN: It's all my mothers. Go for your life. I want you to.

BARBARA: Arigatoo gozaimasu – Jap talk. 'Thank you very much.' [*The tuba*] Jesus. Why is that bloody thing still there?
[BARBARA *stares at the tuba.*]
Does this actually live in the lounge room?

DEN: We lost the case. . . it's probably full of dust. It just stayed. I can't play.

BARBARA: We'll hang on to the furniture until you get promoted.

DEN: Not so much a promotion, Barbara.

BARBARA: And I'm making my way up the ladder. Once I've paid you back. This is Sharalyn at the Academy, 'You keep up your confidence Barbara, and Resort International will not pass you by.' That's how they speak. I don't take any notice.
[*She looks about.*]
And which is going to be my room?

DEN: Well. . . same as mine. I mean where you've. . . where we've. . . when you've been here. My parents' old room. You know, you admired the built-ins. I washed the sheets.

BARBARA: I knew this. You have to let me have a room.
[*Silence.* DEN *has no idea what to say.*]

You know the amount of homework I get, Den. You can't do elocution in the kitchen. This is a professional course. I have to work twice as hard as everyone else. I'm talking about genuine obstacles. You try being short. I'm twice as old as everyone and three times as fat. You can't learn Japanese with another person present. I'm not just mucking around you know.

DEN: [*after a moment*] Well, my old room, if that's what you . . . I'll get rid of all the iron man trophies.

[*Leading* BARBARA *into a room*] I was going to show you when I'd finished it.

[*They step into a 'room'. The tuba plays. This is the room with the model railway.*]

BARBARA: No! This isn't fair. It practically fills the entire room. Your sister's room, where's that? Oh, I knew we should have settled this. I mean –

DEN: It could go back out into the living room.

BARBARA: You're joking. And it's not even a very good one. I mean all those little people all piled up. It looks like that Bopal in India.

DEN: My sister didn't have a room, we had double-bunks in here.

BARBARA: You think something's sorted out. . . I left work on the basis of this. . .

DEN: I realise that, but I just started to work on it again. You might know about the scenery – some of the wives used to take an interest.

BARBARA: I just want some space. I can't have any stress. God, I'd love a smoke, but I won't.

DEN: I'll move the whole thing out.

BARBARA: And no arguments. I can't have any arguments.

DEN: If there's just the half – I'll only work on it when you're out. There's a couple of boom-gates –

BARBARA: Any strain goes straight to my face and stays there.

DEN: Right.

[*Pause*]

Well, we won't. Argue. We won't argue, you just threw me
sort of thing. Not this, but. . .

BARBARA: Not to sleep in. I don't mean to sleep in silly
sausage! It's not as if I'd be sleeping here, is it?
[*She embraces him.*]

DEN: Oh, well. That's all right then.
[*Still embraced, he pulls a yellowing note from his
pocket.*]
Found this when I was clearing up. 'Turn that TV down,
Den's on night shift.' They didn't speak to each other for
years, my parents. 'Can't you eat toast quietly?', all that sort
of thing.

BARBARA: Well, I never shut up so you've got no problems
there.

DEN: I was just starting to look forward to getting up in the
mornings. Not sure if I will now. . .
[*He kisses* BARBARA *on the neck.*]

BARBARA: [*the champagne*] I'll go and stick this in the fridge.
[*She picks up her beauty bag and goes.*]

DEN: 'I've seen flowers come and go in stony places
And kind things done by men with ugly faces
And the gold cup won by the worst horse at the races, so
I trust, too.'
[DEN *picks up the tuba and* BARBARA's *remaining items
and leaves. The roses stay.*]

*The public-speaking class. The sound of a bell and about ten
people applauding, as* DEN *takes his position. He clutches some
small note-cards, looking off at the last speaker. He is very
conscious of not dropping his cards.*

Right. Well, that's something to compete with – not
compete. We're not competing. I meant it's a hard act to
follow. Right. Here I go.
[*His posture and presentation stiffen slightly. He is
conscious that one is meant to look people in the eye for*

*a certain length of time, but this does not come naturally
to him. He does not manage to conquer his nerves, but
forces himself to continue. He has rehearsed it.*]
Right. Well my phrase is 'good on you'. Do I say what it is?
Well I've said it now. You might have heard this before. A
bit of a legend. Apparently. But actually it was my father.
The day he retired from Wongawilli Colliery.
[*He checks his cards and reads out loud*]
'Elaborate.'
[*Pause*]
Yes. . . Ah, yes. He'd been underground since he was a kid.
This was the day of his very last shift. And, what you
probably need to know is that no matter how hard they
worked the coal, how hard they fought for it – no deputy, no
mine-manager had ever said, 'well done, thanks for that.'
[DEN *looks at his card.*]
Sorry. Shower. . . ah, yes. So after he'd had his shower –
and no-one knew how he talked them into it – he got the
staff out of the offices and posed on the step for a photo.
[*He surreptitiously looks at the cards.*]
My mother had an Instamatic which was quite a –
[*He drops the cards. And looks at them there on the floor
at his feet.*]
Right.
[*He decides to battle on. He is conscious of no longer
having the cards to cling to, but he fights his panic.*]
So he's had his shower, and he takes the photo, and as he's
walking through the gate – 'cheers, cheers, see you in the
club of a Friday'. The manager steps forward. Just as he's
going through the gate. And calls out, 'Bert. Thank you for
everything. You've done a very good job. Good on you.'
And the old man, father, turned around, opened his mouth
to give his final words, fell straight down in the dirt and
literally had a stroke. 'Good work' and wham. [*Laughing*]
Literally had a stroke.

[*This is not the hit he had hoped it would be. His class has not got the joke.*]

It's not as if he died. He thought it was very funny, himself. Once he learnt to speak again he used to tell the story. Nearly gave himself another one laughing about it. [*Smiling as he sits*] Actually, I thought some of you might have heard it before. I didn't mean to shock anyone. Sorry. Different circles I suppose. That's just mines. Before they brought in bonuses. . .

[*Bright lights fading*]

Mines. . . and small lives. . .

BARBARA *enters with a pad and pen, and marches straight to* DEN. *She thrusts them in his hands, as if for the umpteenth time, sits him in the chair and stands with her back to him. Her frustration, not to mention her high heels, is killing her. She is paying even more attention to her grooming, perhaps having taken on yet another style of dressing. The purpose of the exercise is for her to explain, with patience, an object for drawing, with her back to the person sketching. It is intended to place emphasis on verbal skills.*

BARBARA: Well, open your ear holes. Listen. For god's sake. Draw two squashed circles sort of away from the whole thing and draw two lines from both the circles –

DEN: Upwards or downwards?

BARBARA: No! No!

[*She marches back to* DEN *and grabs the paper.*]

Downwards. Downwards. A ship's two funnels. It was meant to be a ship. A ship. That's not a ship. That's not anything like I said. Is it Den.

DEN: You're supposed to be a bit clearer. Poised.

BARBARA: Well, excuse me. How can I help it if you can't draw.

DEN: You're supposed to explain it calmly. That seems to be the exercise. Not whether I draw the boat right or not.

BARBARA: Look I had this all day thank you very much. You see how you like it – in a state of siege the entire day. They were the same as you. All out to sabotage me. Brainless pack of sheilas. In the end she says, 'We have to move onto self-esteem, but Barbara. . . ', 'Ye-es, Cassandra,' 'Perhaps you'd like another go tomorrow. When we've got the video so you can have a little look at yourself.'

DEN: This is very good for you.

[*As she turns, ready to start again*]

BARBARA: Tell me something I don't know. Right. [*She turns around.*] Now, draw a line across the top of the page, but it doesn't really reach the ends. Now draw- [*She turns*] Why didn't you start a new page! I mean – oh for god's sake, fuck me dead with a rissole, I shouldn't have to tell you to start a new page! Turn the page! Turn the page!

[VERGE *has entered. She carries one bag.* BARBARA *stands stock still.*]

VERGE: I'm wrecked. How was I meant to find you. It could have been an emergency. I wouldn't have started if I'd known – it's been very bloody hard. Don't think it hasn't. I'm right, I got off the right train. The taxi was parked where you get off so I didn't have to wave all over the roadside. I went to that [*She checks her hand where her notes are written.*] that Buena Vista place but they were all stupid. So I said to the taxi we'd go to . . . to your old house and Barry, says, he says, she lives somewhere else now. Turn up the books or something. I didn't know what he was talking about. I actually want my mother, actually Barry. And he says I'll drive you, and his breath all had beer on it. Under oh-five and stay alive. No thank you. So I say the taxi's still here I can manage. So he looks up the phone book and writes down the address. Something or other Bethlehem Street. I tell the driver who was quite nice and he can't read the number either. Drunk writing. I'm fed up but I have to knock on all these doors. Do you know where my mother lives? Speak English why don't you. And the driver's

waiting and I'm cross – and lucky for me you started
screaming. There she is. So.

[*Pause*]

Nice house. [*To* DEN] Excuse me dear, the taxi-driver's
waiting to get paid.

DEN: Right.

[DEN, *completely lost, checks his wallet and goes.*]

VERGE: [*pause*] Yes.

[*Pause*]

It was a bit of a rough trip. You look a bit different.

[*One of* BARBARA's *worst nightmares.*]

BARBARA: Dear god in heaven what do you think you're doing
here. Did Marj send you here? You don't just up and –
what's that bag got in it?

[*Pause*]

Did she send you here?

VERGE: [*mumbling*] My idea.

BARBARA: What?

VERGE: Beg your pardon Mrs Mardon.

[*Pause*]

It was my idea. I wanted to. I've got a headache from
tension. And no sign of a bowel movement. Tension.
Travelling.

BARBARA: Does matron know where you are?

VERGE: I don't even know where I am.

BARBARA: We'll have to ring her.

VERGE: It's all right, thank you. I don't have to go back.
Anyway I'm too old.

BARBARA: Did you bring your medication?

VERGE: I'm off it. I'm meant to be. I'm just a bit fed up at the
moment. [*To* DEN *as he returns with more suitcases*] I'm
calming down. Look.

BARBARA: This is Den. Den my friend. This is Virginia.

VERGE: Verge. Verge. Verge. 'Your daughter', say.

BARBARA: My daughter.

VERGE: How do you do, Den, it's very nice to meet you. [*She wipes her hands very thoroughly and shakes his.*] This is quite nice. Boyfriend or just friend, if you don't mind my asking?

DEN: Boyfriend.

  [*Pause*]

  You're a bit of a surprise.

VERGE: That's me – surprising. Aren't I? Mum?

  [*Pause*]

  Barbara? [*To* DEN] I always pay back money.

BARBARA: It's not like her to go wandering off.

VERGE: I'm not wandering. I came down here. I meant to. To
  . . . doesn't matter.

BARBARA: Did something happen. Perhaps if she speaks to Marj.
  On the phone.

VERGE: [*to* DEN] Everyone else has got these mothers.

BARBARA: Come off it, you want for nothing.

DEN: [*to* VERGE] I beg your pardon?

VERGE: [*still to* DEN] At the workshop. They live at home with
  their mothers. Never shut up about them.

BARBARA: She's always needed proper attention.

VERGE: I go back to live at Merry Meadows I'll just go insane.

BARBARA: Stop calling it Merry Meadows. [*To* DEN] It's not
  called that at all.

VERGE: Sunny farm.

BARBARA: Sunshine Hostel.

VERGE: Funny farm.

BARBARA: She's always liked it there.

VERGE: I've stopped.

BARBARA: I'll take her back up tomorrow.

VERGE: I don't belong there.

  [*Pause.* VERGE *sits down on her cases.*]

BARBARA: Tell the truth. Did Marj put you on that train?

VERGE: I belong with you. No, silly.

BARBARA: She needs supervision. I can't look after you.

VERGE: Shut up, I don't!

DEN: [*their temperament*] I can see a bit of a resemblance.

BARBARA: Oh for god's sake. Look. Look at these scars.

> [BARBARA *pulls up* VERGE'*s top to reveal burn marks and scars from self-inflicted injuries, they are also on her arms,* BARBARA *cannot get her to roll up her sleeves.*]

VERGE: Stop it. So what?

BARBARA: [*to* DEN] See? I'm not being heartless.

VERGE: [*to* DEN] I don't do it anymore. I can't even remember . . . I was little. . .

BARBARA: You still are, you just don't think you are.

VERGE: I am not settled.

BARBARA: [*pause*] Marj and I talked about community housing. That sounds very nice.

VERGE: Don't be funny. Who with? I don't like anyone and no-one likes me. They're stupid, they can't even think. They're just – pathetic.

DEN: All right. . .

BARBARA: Marj has got a room all set up for her.

VERGE: Full of all these fluffy animals. I wrote to you and told you. I never once said I liked fluffy animals. Put it full of boys and I might like going there. [*To* DEN] Why not? I'm a single girl.

BARBARA: Christ.

VERGE: You know, Den, how I've been working in this workshop.

DEN: No. No. I don't know anything about you.

BARBARA: Let her get on with it.

DEN: No point saying yes, if I don't.

BARBARA: And that's right, you can't miss work. They're relying on you to. . . to. . . [*Unsure*] pack the dental floss or whatever it is.

VERGE: Well, guess what. They gave me the sack.

BARBARA: Say that again.

VERGE: Say that again. They gave me the sack.

BARBARA: [*to* DEN] They can't sack people in a sheltered workshop.

VERGE: They don't like you swearing at the supervisors.

BARBARA: Then don't.

VERGE: It's boiling hot, you could die.

BARBARA: The others work there happily.

VERGE: [*nearly shouting*] Well I think I must be different!

BARBARA: [*to herself*] A voice that could cut glass.

VERGE: [*to* DEN] Mrs Bartlett says, 'I don't think your own mother could love you.'

DEN: That's a bit rough.

BARBARA: She'll have to go to Marj's.

VERGE: [*to* DEN] Marj is bad for my nerves. I won't. We go somewhere like the shops and she says stuff to people, I don't know them. 'She's coming on.' I can't stand it.

[BARBARA *puts her hands on* VERGE'*s waist, holds her and looks directly into her eyes.* VERGE *starts touching* BARBARA'*s blouse, loving this contact with her mother.*]

BARBARA: Listen carefully. There's no room here, Verge. For you to move here it would have had to be planned. Well in advance.

[VERGE *strokes* BARBARA'*s face.*]

VERGE: I love you.

BARBARA: They let them watch too much television, that much is obvious.

[*Pause*]

I love you, but you can't stay.

[*Silence.* VERGE *begins to inch her bags into the room.* BARBARA *takes off her heels.*]

DEN: We'll find some room for you.

BARBARA: No! This is a crucial stage in my life.

[VERGE *runs in to the living room and sets down her bags.*]

VERGE: [*to* DEN] OK. Good. I kept hoping and dreaming and hoping and dreaming and –

BARBARA: She'll be bored to tears. No-one's got to time to keep you entertained. You can't. Let's not put Den in a difficult position.

[*Pause*]

It's not that I don't want you. [*Pause, then to* DEN] You explain it to her. I'll be right back, I'm going to get some smokes.

[VERGE *might be wiping away tears of joy. Silence.*]

DEN: Right.

VERGE: I'm OK. Yes, thank you Den. Lovely place. Gorgeous.

[*Pause*]

She didn't really mean it. . .

DEN: Well, I hate to say it but I think she did.

VERGE: I'm just a bit of a surprise.

DEN: [*laughs*] You're a shock, I don't know about a surprise. You're a bolt from the blue.

VERGE: [*laughs*] Her heart's quite strong though.

DEN: I'll get you some blankets.

VERGE: I just need security. It was in my file and it's true. Somewhere I belong. And no bullshit.

DEN: Blankets and no bullshit. Fair enough.

[DEN *picks up her cases and starts to go.*]

VERGE: I'm not stupid. [*Mumbling*] A bit slow, maybe. . .

DEN: Oh well, we're all a bit slow round here – you go for your life.

VERGE: [*spelling it out*] Just a bit slow to catch on. Sparks in the brain.

DEN: [*as he goes, smiling*] I was complaining that my life was dull.

[VERGE *and* DEN *go off in search of blankets.*]

END OF ACT ONE

ACT TWO

A small light goes on. It is a miner's helmet, RON *is fishing on the point.* DEN *sits for a while then he is up again fossicking around for* RON's *lost watch. He also wears a helmet. Sounds of lapping water and the occasional speeding car.*

RON: Look, mate. Listen. It doesn't matter.
  [*But* DEN *continues to search.*]
DEN: A good watch like that. . .
RON: It's a cheap watch, someone'll find it who'll be glad of it.
  [DEN *stands, uncertain.*]
  Look, from memory, half the pleasure of this is in just sitting and being still. Are you sure you don't want a go?
  [DEN *sits.*]
DEN: If you could guarantee I wouldn't catch anything.
  [DEN *puts his hand in a bucket and plays with some little fish.*]
RON: Keep this quiet, but we've been ask to target another fifty. To go.
  [*Pause*]
DEN: I suppose we've got all those blokes on light duties.
  [*Pause*]
  Half the time their injuries get worse, the sort of things they're given to do.
RON: I told them there wasn't any need, of course.
DEN: Oh. Right. Just thinking out loud.
RON: Accountants wanting their quarterly figures up, talk about a mind-set.
  [*Pause*]

DEN: The retraining hasn't fallen through? Going for my welders ticket – is that still on the cards?

RON: Oh yeah. Yeah. I'd just be going a bit easy if I were you.

DEN: [*justifying*] We had to refuse to send those panels down. They were well and truly out.

RON: You've stopped the line three days running.

DEN: Not me. The team. It was what we were told [*. . . To do*]

RON: All right. Fair enough.

DEN: Unless I've missed something.

RON: No, no. You're right.

DEN: Right.

RON: I'm just saying, go easy.

DEN: If we want to get that tooling sorted out. . . [*. . . Then it's what we have to do*]

RON: Just – [*He stops himself.*] we've been asked to stop what we're doing and write a forward projection, a little story about what happens next. Great timing – you start to get a bit of rapport going. . .

[*Pause*]

DEN: Could've been going a bit too fast. That'd be it.

[*Pause*]

Or something to do with this China contract.

[RON *stands and tugs at his line angrily.*]

RON: What the hell's wrong with this place? There always used to be fish here, always. When I was a kid, I never once fished here and went home without a feed.

[RON *reels in his line and collects his things.*]

I'm serious about this. Don't hold things up – not any more than is necessary. [*Reassuring him*] You're all right, but just for the moment

[DEN *is reassured. The tuba.* RON *starts to clamber over the rocks,* DEN *begins to follow. The miners' helmets go out.*]

VERGE *is in the room with the model railway. The scenery [people, buildings etc] has been arranged in a fashion. There is*

a large rolling hill with buildings perched perilously on top.
VERGE *is having the time of her life. She calls out to* DEN.
VERGE: Hey Den! Hey Den! Hey Den, hey Den, hey Den, hey
   Den! I didn't even know what a village looked like!
      [DEN *is in [for him] beachwear. He is lost, looking for*
      BARBARA. *He looks at the railway. And smiles.*]
DEN: That's right. Like a dog's breakfast. That's right.
VERGE: [*laughing*] Den. . .
DEN: You do whatever you like.
      [*In his pocket he has some little coloured packets.*]
   Now with this scatter material you've got oak and sycamore,
   dead and fallen, autumn leaves and rotten foliage. Go easy
   on the rotten foliage.
VERGE: But Den.
      [*She puts down the scenery.*]
   So in this dream – I'm in this dream and there was a –
   catastrophe.
DEN: I suppose you were responsible.
VERGE: And there were people running everywhere. And cars all
   – everyone driving everywhere. And everyone trying to get
   out of the. . .
DEN: Catastrophe.
VERGE: So then, I think, what are they doing? And I go and
   stand in the middle. Great mess. Stop! And everyone says,
   who said that, Frank? All right – this is me – you can go.
   Now you. Now stop. Come on. Stop. I'm warning you. . . I
   even made an ambulance wait. Den, you're not kidding, I
   would love, l-o-v-e love to be a organiser. Just organising.
      [*Pause*]
DEN: Not a lot of call for organisers.
VERGE: What?
DEN: That was a dream.
VERGE: But being a disco-dancer, that's not a dream. Or being
   Torville and Dean. I could be.
DEN: No.
VERGE: Marj goes, 'You can't even ice-skate.'

DEN: That's right.

VERGE: Just not being anything?

DEN: You can just be here. For the present. That's all you have to do.

[*She blows a kiss.*]

VERGE: I love you.

[*Pause*]

DEN: You've been watching too much television.

[*She laughs, deposits the section of the model and goes off to get some more.*]

DEN *laughs and sees* RON. *It is as if he has been caught out by* DEN *as he moves out of the plant.*

RON: They're moving us out for a while – to some offices in town. Paperwork. . . you know. Speaking of which, Jeannie wants me to come up and look at the house. I don't know what she's on about but she's getting a valuation. Reckons she hadn't heard from you. And it's about time I met this Barbara, I mean all right she may be shy. . . but still. . .

[DEN *watches* RON *go.*]

DEN *wanders off in search of* BARBARA. *It is Sunday at the nearly completed International hotel. The Fool on the Hill is playing – muzak version. The tape is broken – it stops halfway and starts again. All day.* BARBARA *enters, running as well as she is able in high heeled sandals, and stepping over building debris. She wears a highly co-ordinated casual outfit.* DEN *enters. He stands on the periphery.* BARBARA's *vowels are occasionally more rounded.*

DEN: Well. I didn't know where you'd got to. [*Looking around*] Still a bit of a mess. They've got a bit of a way to go. To get it opened in time.

BARBARA: They know what they're doing Den. I mean they've done it in other parts of the world. Listen.

DEN: [*listening*] Before it's open. . .

[BARBARA *looks around.*]

BARBARA: Of course they'll bring the plants in fully grown. These days it's all in the landscaping. Bring them in already blooming.

DEN: I wouldn't have thought you could just wander around. [*Looks back*] You don't think we've sort of broken in. . . ?

BARBARA: The cars'll all pull in here. [*The circular driveway*]

DEN: The picnic's still over on the beach.

BARBARA: Piped music – and still got some of the scaffolding up. I mean. . . [*Reading*] Resort Beach International Hotel. Small letters. It's all they need.

DEN: I put the umbrella down in case the wind picks up. Fly around, stab someone through the chest, you'd never forgive yourself. The picnic things are still on the beach.

BARBARA: You said that.

[BARBARA *swans about the space.*]

Our guests come in this entrance – won't they know they're somewhere. They've. . . arrived. Of course the calibre of guest. Nice. People who expect to be treated well. So what do they do? Treat other people well.

DEN: Barbara – something to remember –

[*She stands still, not looking at him.*]

You haven't got the job yet.

BARBARA: For the umpteenth time, the Academy knows the personnel manager. We're being channelled.

DEN: So you've got a very good chance.

BARBARA: Den, I ask you. Look at me.

[*She gives* DEN *a demonstration of one of her walking 'turns'. She is still for a moment, looking at* DEN, *then notices something.*]

Oh. Look. That'd be the atrium.

[*She steps over rubble and* DEN *follows her, he stands behind her, and then she begins to guide his hand down the outside of her thigh. She leans back on him. Licks his fingers.*]

Salt. Lovely.

DEN: I'll just duck over and get the vinegar.

[BARBARA *is gazing into the hotel.*]

BARBARA: I love it when you pursue me.

DEN: I don't know that I ever do.

BARBARA: You don't. Go on. . .

[*He does, standing behind her and caressing her.*]

Oh, Den. Marble. It's all marble. [*She guides his hand.*] I
thought it would be – smooth, no edges. Marble. Those big
soft brown mops that open and close that just glide around,
catching every piece of nothing. People slinking. Sliding
down marble walls. It's soothing, marble. Put your face
against it. I would like to lie stretched out on that marble
floor.

[*She places his hand on her inner thigh.*]

Not to show off, not when anyone was there. For myself.
Don't stop.

DEN: I – er. Right.

BARBARA: You're supposed to know.

[*She turns and they kiss. Then back to the hotel. After a
little difficulty baring her shoulder, he kisses it.*]

I knew it! I told you! Over there. Sails outside to shield the
guests from the sun. They move, I read about it. Design. 'No
madam. Please don't change tables. I'll get – *arrange* for
someone to adjust the sails.' Stop – Listen, and Respond
Appropriately. [DEN *stops*] Not you. Oh god.

[*She drops to her haunches.* DEN *behind her.*]

When they arrive at reception, look. . . they see straight
through to the surf.

DEN: [*looking in the same direction*] There goes the umbrella.

[BARBARA *does not laugh. They get comfortable.*]

BARBARA: [*smiling at* DEN] You should have brought the towels
over. . . Somewhere to ourselves. That's what I've been
needing.

DEN: Right. That feel nice?

BARBARA: You're supposed to know – yes. Oh god, I want this
so much.

[BARBARA *continues to look in the hotel,* DEN *is unsure of quite what she means.*]

DEN: [*pause*] I'm game if you are.

BARBARA: You know what, Den.

DEN: What, honey?

BARBARA: You never see cleaners in places like this. They've probably got tunnels for them running under the floor.

DEN: Don't you worry, I wouldn't let them give you a cleaning job.

BARBARA: Oh well, shit.

[*She leaps up.*]

Den you tell me why you said that. What possesses you to say things like that? God. I'll have my diploma. I'll have you know I'm going to pass, Den. I'm not mucking around. What do I have to do to prove I'm not mucking around?

DEN: I know. Come here.

BARBARA: You don't go through the rigours of that course to attain a rotten old cleaning job. What'd you say that for? What on earth did you say that for? I mean if that's really what you think of me – oh, I don't know what to make of this.

DEN: Nothing. I don't mean anything.

[*Pause*]

Would you really like me to go and get the towels? We could go just over there.

[*Pause*]

I wish you could see yourself – you look lovely.

BARBARA: Afternoon light, only sort I look any good in.

DEN: I'm going to get the towels, and you'll be here when I get back. . .

[*He nods to the chosen position.*]

Who'd know?

BARBARA: Just us. Me! I'd know. Outside my hotel, when the crane was still on the roof.

[*As he goes*]

It'll give me an aura when I go for the interview. Eh, talk
about an intimate knowledge of the hotel trade.

[DEN *smiles and moves off to get the towels.*]

Den – the next instalment of fees are due.

[*Pause*]

I'm worth it.

DEN: I thought you might be.

BARBARA: What we have to do is be proud of each other. . .
And have faith.

VERGE *leaps up and runs across the hill area. She has a pair of
binoculars around her neck. The sound of a coal truck is heard.*

VERGE: Here they come! Here they come! Oh god, I knew it! I
just did. A flock of wandering tattlers.

[*She lets the binoculars hang, closes her eyes and
pretends to be a tree.* DEN *arrives behind her.*]

Ssssh. They're probably going to land on me.

DEN: [*to himself, smiling*] I've created a monster.

VERGE: See if you can look like a tree, Den.

DEN: It's rocks they come here for. Those rocky islands.
They've got enough trees at home.

VERGE: All the way from. . .

DEN: [*going along with her*] Alaska and Siberia.

VERGE: Miles and miles and miles away. Where there's snow.
I can see them, I can. Flying all the way here just to get
warm.

[*Pause*]

The people at home don't know they've gone. [*Looking at*
DEN] Oh god, that's shocking. . .

DEN: They know, the people at home.

VERGE: Just frantic because they've disappeared.

DEN: No, no. They know they'll come back.

VERGE: Every year – do they come here every year?

DEN: Yes.

VERGE: Will I see them next year too? Would I still be here to see them then?

[*She rounds on him with the binoculars.*]

You dare just say 'yes', mister, and you'll get it.

DEN: I don't know, no bullshit.

VERGE: Oh I wish. I wish I wish I wish I wish. Den –

DEN: How would you go being quiet for a minute?

VERGE: Den, the ones who get here last of the flock. What if – what if Den, they're so late the others have had their summer, and are just about to go back. The late ones – do they, I wonder, just rest and go home late – or do the not late birds give them a ride on their wings?

[*Pause*]

DEN: No, the early birds shoot them for convenience, before they start the homeward run.

[*Pause*]

VERGE: What will happen to me? If. . .

[DEN *looks at her.*]

If your father wants his binoculars back?

DEN: I told you – he's dead. They're a present from me.

VERGE: He used to watch for the tattlers.

DEN: [*laughs*] No. He'd come up here and look down at the steelworks, at their stockpile of coal. And if it was high, sometime that week the undermanager'd make sure there was a strike. But these days, it's a bit more sophisticated. If someone in Tokyo didn't like his lunch, he might shut them down for good.

VERGE: He was a cranky old bugger.

DEN: Yes.

VERGE: A cranky old bugger with binoculars.

DEN: And he would've liked you. Not that you'd ever have guessed.

VERGE: Say – what would happen to me? If you and Barbara really had that baby. Like soon?

DEN: These things take time. . .

VERGE: But could I stay? To help?

DEN: Well, there's a lot of work in a baby, you could be our servant.

VERGE: Slave.

DEN: That's the shot. Slave.

VERGE: The job you're getting you'll have tons of money.

[*She dances past* DEN *and puts out her hand for a coin.*]

DEN: Now you've made it a family tradition, except my father only ever gave me threepence.

VERGE: Quinquereme of Ninevah from distant Ophir,
Rowing home to – to –

DEN: Haven.

VERGE: Haven in Sunny Palestine. When I came here I couldn't hardly remember even one song.

DEN: Well, go on.

VERGE: With a cargo of ivory, And apes and peacocks,

DEN & VERGE: Sandalwood, cedarwood and sweet white wine.

VERGE: Second verse. Stately Spanish galleon coming from the Isthmus,
Dipping through the tropics by the palm-green shores,
With a cargo of diamonds, emeralds, amethysts, topazes and cinnamon, and gold moidores.

DEN: You know you were looking at pigeons up there.

VERGE: Yes. I knew.

[*They both leave to prepare for a party.*]

Party music. The concrete terrace at the back of DEN's *house. There is a string of coloured lights and they flash.* BARBARA *is a little tipsy. She has a drink for herself and one for* RON. RON, *on* JEANNIE's *orders, is crawling around under the house looking at the foundations. Suddenly the music becomes very loud.*

BARBARA: [*calling*] I don't think so! Den tell her to get out of it, she's had her fun. [*The lights*] Utterly hopeless. Honestly.

[*The lights continue to flash.*]

[*Calling*] I thought you said these worked.

[*The lights continue to flash.* DEN *enters.*]
It's a barbecue, Den. Not the Lion's Club annual picnic. You
didn't say they flashed.

DEN: You didn't ask.

BARBARA: Looks like every Maltese wedding I've never been to.
[*Whispering*] Can you tell me what that man is doing down
there?

[DEN *is silent*]

[*Calling*] Beer's getting flat, Ron. [*To* DEN] I mean, have a
look around the house by all means, but I wouldn't have
thought he'd be wanting to clamber under the foundations.

DEN: Oh well. He's family.

BARBARA: [*looking off*] The flyscreen door! They'll be trooping
all over the salad.

DEN: [*popping back in*] Great job on the food. I said he'd like
you.

[*The music is turned up again.*]

BARBARA: No thank you! I said no, thank you!
[*She is about to march off and break the stereo when* RON
emerges from under the house. He has a torch.]
Everything all right down there? We're not in any danger of
sliding down the hill, Ron? We're not going to end up eating
our dinner in number four blast furnace?

RON: I beg your pardon, I have been down there a while. . .

BARBARA: Well of course, I twigged. Exploration, I know.
Where Den's dad kept all his *Playboys*, isn't it? Down
below?

RON: No.

BARBARA: Pulling your leg!

RON: It's an ideal space for another room. An extension.

BARBARA: Well there's an idea. I was just saying to Den that we
need a bit more space – an entertainment area sort of thing.
[*The beer*] Here you go. Of course, you don't want to over-
capitalise.

[BARBARA *endeavours to relax. The music is turned up.*]

Thank you! I have asked once! Oh, my head's full of plans for this place.

RON: That right?

BARBARA: We won't be here forever of course Ron – don't our lives turn round? [*Quieter*] Ron, I don't know what you've been doing, but that Den of mine has a new lease of life.

RON: You've had a bit to do with that.

BARBARA: Oh, yes well, between the two of us.

[*She checks that* DEN *is out of earshot.*]

The man had given up on himself. I couldn't cope at first. I mean nice chap, but. . .

[RON *kills a mosquito.*]

Oh, aren't they enormous. We'll all come down with that Ross River fever. And what a wonderful position you have, Ron.

RON: Plenty of variety.

BARBARA: And let's face it, and I don't think it's an ugly word – you're in a position of power. Den tells me his works'll be jumping. [*Listens, surprised*] Is that the door?

RON: Ultimately it's all up to the Department. . . and market forces. . .

BARBARA: Right Ron, just before [*She looks for* DEN.] I think it's marvellous that he's picking up a trade, his welder's ticket, [*Laughing*] I don't think it's ever too late. But wasn't there something more like. . . plumbing? You know – electricians. I mean look at what they charge.

RON: No decisions have been made.

BARBARA: That's right. And it's not as if the PR scene isn't keeping me on my toes.

[*As* DEN *enters*]

Den you know what we should have? The trees outside the International have got them. Nice touch. The tiniest little white lights.

RON: The Resort Beach White Elephant. Pink Elephant.

[*Silence*]

BARBARA: Don't you think that they're sophisticated? Den? Those lights.

RON: Oh, I hope your firm's not involved in the opening day extravaganza?

[DEN *looks at* BARBARA – *what firm?* BARBARA *shakes her head.*]

BARBARA: [*quietly*] No. I can't say my PR firm is involved.

RON: It'll be a good place to stay away from next week.

BARBARA: No. Not next week. I don't think so.

RON: Or the week after, whatever – there's a ten page supplement in the paper this morning.

BARBARA: It's a rag that paper. Full of shit always has been. [*To* DEN] It's ages away.

[BARBARA *is trying to smile when* VERGE *enters dancing to the music. She wears an item or two of* BARBARA'*s and carries a plate full of savouries – jatz adorned with gherkins etc.*]

VERGE: Isn't it great having functions? It's just great.

BARBARA: I'll take those. Off you go.

[VERGE *looks at the lights.*]

RON: We wondered where you'd got to.

BARBARA: Thanks. [*To* VERGE] Off you go.

VERGE: [*pointing to* BARBARA. *Confidentially to* RON] She left me, but now we're back together.

BARBARA: Dear, I wish she'd stop saying that. [*Mouthing*] Having a little holiday. Who was at the door?

VERGE: No-one. Ron, you know Kelvin Pearce?

RON: [*slight pause. Smiling*] Oh yes. I think I do.

BARBARA: Give me those jatz. Cocktail onions and Coon. Weeklies from the sixties, kitchen's full of them.

VERGE: Kelvin Pearce wouldn't be able to look at those lights because he's an epileptic.

BARBARA: Well aren't we lucky Kelvin Pearce isn't here?

VERGE: Ron. Bullshit you know Kelvin Pearce.

[*She goes to* DEN. RON *flounders.*]

RON: Kelvin. Sorry thought you said Kevin

BARBARA: Poor Den, instant family – just for the moment.

DEN: Let's see how that fire's going.

VERGE: Watch!

[VERGE *dances and trips. The savouries go flying off.* VERGE *is shocked.*]

BARBARA: I think I warned her. Gherkin stains all over the concrete.

[*She leaves* VERGE *on the ground picking up the jatz.* DEN *helps her. The music is turned off.*]

DEN: They looked pretty colourful, flying through the air. Eh, Ron?

RON: I've never seen anything like it.

VERGE: [*to* RON] Shut up.

RON: [*quietly to* DEN] Barbara's saying you've got plans for this place?

[VERGE *leaps up.* BARBARA *enters carrying a broom. With* MARJ, *who is smiling awkwardly.*]

MARJ: She opened the door, told me I had the wrong house, and – and closed it again. I couldn't make anyone hear, above the music.

BARBARA: Verge, this is very intriguing. Marj tells me you're off down the – coast for the weekend.

[VERGE *is silent.*]

MARJ: We arranged it last week, she said that she'd asked your permission. That you'd. . . [. . . *said yes*]

BARBARA: Very sorry, Ron. Someone's got their wires crossed here. My sister Marj. Ron. And Den. Well, now you can meet Den.

[*Before* MARJ *gets a chance to shake hands with* RON, *or acknowledge* DEN.]

VERGE: People keep walking on the savouries!

MARJ: [*to* RON] I won't be a moment. This is – rather embarrassing.

VERGE: [*to* MARJ] I said no.

MARJ: You gave me directions, when I told you I was coming down. So you must have wanted to come along.

VERGE: No, no!

[*Beat*]

MARJ: In fact, Barbara, she said she had to get special permission because you had forbidden her to speak to me. [*To* RON] I am sorry.

BARBARA: Not that I recall. [*To* RON] We'll eat in a moment. I am sorry. [*To* MARJ] She's not going anywhere she doesn't want to go.

[RON *moves to the periphery.* DEN *sweeps around their feet.*]

MARJ: I rented a car. Especially. [*To* VERGE] You said you thought it would be nice –

VERGE: [*thrusting a clipping at* MARJ] Mum graduated and her photo was in the paper.

BARBARA: [*snatching it*] I don't think we want to flaunt my success.

MARJ: Just for the weekend. I'm going to bring you back. You know that.

BARBARA: All my life I've had this. [DEN *sweeping*] That's enough!

MARJ: Had what? [*To the men*] I am sorry. . .

VERGE: Oh god! Oh god! Don't make me go!

[VERGE *clings to the broom.*]

BARBARA: That's right. Give the neighbours an earful.

DEN: Look, she doesn't want to go. . .

MARJ: She tells me that she hasn't been doing anything.

VERGE: Who's she? I wonder who she is?

MARJ: Hanging around shopping centres is hardly an activity, is it? She told me very proudly that she goes to K-Mart every day.

VERGE: Well? Someone has to!

MARJ: I am simply offering to take her on a nice little trip. [*To* BARBARA] Come along if you like.

BARBARA: She doesn't want to go.

MARJ: My god, Barbara, you're wilful.

VERGE: Please no! Please no!

[*Pause*]

DEN: Look. It's very nice of you, but it might be best if you
. . . We're looking after her. Or she's looking after herself.
So you have a safe trip. I probably don't look like much to
you, but I'm steady. [*Smiling*] Pay-packets guaranteed for a
while. So she's all right here. That's what I'm saying.

[BARBARA *has arranged herself so that the three of them
present as a family.*]

BARBARA: She doesn't think you're human if you live down
here.

MARJ: Oh, that is not true.

BARBARA: But things are really picking up. [*To* RON] A rocket
up some stodgy old arses really does the trick.

MARJ: Graduated from what?

BARBARA: So afraid I'll have things better than you.

MARJ: I was only showing some interest!

DEN: I know you mean well, but we are managing all right. As
a family.

BARBARA: And we're in the middle of a celebration, Den's new
career. [*To* DEN] Not that she'd think it was anything much.

MARJ: I'd just hate to think that she was slipping backwards.

DEN: I don't think you'll find anyone slipping backwards.

MARJ: Have you really forbidden her to speak to me? [*To* DEN]
I don't know if you realise, but after all I've done, at my
own expense.

BARBARA: God, I love a martyr.

DEN: That's enough. That's enough. I won't have all this.

MARJ: Dear God, I'd love to know what I've done to you.
You've got a very short memory, I can tell you that right
now – the number of times I've put myself out for you. [*To*
VERGE] And you. Tell me what I've done. I've obviously
stepped on someone's toes.

BARBARA: [*to* RON] She's mad as a cut snake, always has been -

DEN: You heard what I had to say.

[*Pause*]

BARBARA: [*to* VERGE] Come and wave good-bye to your Auntie
Marj.

[BARBARA *and* VERGE *head off.*]

MARJ: [*to* DEN] It's not as if I'm asking for gratitude –

[*Silence.* MARJ *leaves. Silence between* RON *and* DEN.]

DEN: I should bring those lights in. . . probably a bit much.

[*Pause*]

Just can't remember a time when those two weren't here.

RON: This 'celebration' business, all these plans. . .

DEN: [*smiling*] Barbara. . .

RON: You know I've been giving this job my best shot.

[DEN *starts to pick up the rest of the savouries.*]

DEN: Never seen anyone work as hard. All that pressure and you
don't go under.

RON: Because you realise that what we're doing now is just
getting a report out.

[DEN *stands still. Silence.*]

Anyway, that's my problem. I'll go and . . . put the meat on.

[*He takes the plate out of* DEN'S *hand and goes.* DEN
knows he should ask, and doesn't. He watches him go.]

RON *remains on the periphery which becomes dimmer as* VERGE
re-enters to help bring down the lights.

VERGE: Den. Third verse. Dirty *British* coaster with a salt-caked
smoke-stack,

Butting through the Channel in the mad March days;

DEN & VERGE: With a cargo of Tyne coal,

Road rail, pig-lead,

Firewood, iron-ware. . .

RON: . . . and cheap tin-trays.

[DEN *looks to* RON *who disappears.* VERGE *goes off in a
different direction.*]

The public speaking class. DEN *is in the middle of his speech, the final class in the course.*

DEN: So they came to my father – and as I said, he only told me this one story, at my twenty-first birthday tea. Which came out of how he'd had to eat dog on his twenty-first. Six foot four and seven stone. Anyway, sorry. Off the track. [*He looks at his notes.*] So they came to my father, because he was the one who carried the messages, between our officers and theirs. And they said, 'Give us the names of the sickest men, sorry the sickest fifty men and we'll send them to our Japanese hospital'. At this stage they were at one hundred kilo camp along the Burma Railway – one hundred kilometres in. Down to three-quarters of a cup of rice a day.

    [*Pause*]

And his best friend had this bad ulcer that exposed his shin-bone, knee to ankle, and he begged my father, 'Is my name on the list? Put my name on the list.' But the old – father – said no, there were others worse than him. Then the next day they said, 'Send fifty more', and he kept begging and refused to speak to my father unless he got on the list. He was in agony, as you could imagine. But there were fifty others in agony. So that was the end of their friendship. And the night before the second lot went my father thought about this hospital. Where was it, sort of thing. Where could it be. But he'd been having a row with some of his officers, so he kept his doubts to himself. Two months later, news spread through the camp – those one hundred men had been abandoned, twenty miles back down the track, without food or water. A couple of them still alive. After that he became a man who always spoke his mind.

    [*Pause*]

Right. I hope that was all right. Thanks very much. [*Smiling*] I wouldn't say I enjoyed it, but, if you'd have me back next term. . .

    [*Sound of applause*]

BARBARA *has locked herself in the bathroom,* DEN *is outside. She has a newspaper and a pen. Her clothes are tizzy.* DEN *is outside the door.* BARBARA *is closing her eyes and concentrating on each number before she writes on her lotto form, and has taken up smoking again.*

BARBARA: Eighteen.

[*Pause*]

Thirty-six.

[*Pause*]

Well, you have bloody upset me.

DEN: I should be able to ask.

BARBARA: Four.

DEN: Marriage was probably too strong a word. More a question of where I stand.

BARBARA: Outside the bathroom door at the moment. Sixteen.

[*Pause*]

Three.

DEN: Did you know that even if you play Lotto every single day you can only expect to win once every ten thousand years.

BARBARA: Well, I've got something to look forward to then.

[*Pause*]

DEN: Come out of there.

[*Pause*]

All I meant was in a crisis would we stick together, sort of thing.

BARBARA: I'm in one. [*She makes a mistake on her form.*] Shit.

DEN: Just to be sure of something. All sorts of rumours flying around work. . . I mean I am supporting the three of us –

[*Short silence.* BARBARA *picks up her things and strides into the room.*]

BARBARA: Well that's easily solved, Den. Look, she'll listen to you. Tell her she can't stay. She's ruining everything – you just can't see it going on. I do not need this tension. She never stops following me.

DEN: If she wasn't here would it be different between us?

BARBARA: Like it was before. Promise.

DEN: Well. She won't be here forever. But a kid of our own, that'd be different. Wouldn't it?

[BARBARA *looks at* DEN, *somewhat horrified.*]

BARBARA: It'd be smaller I suppose.

[*Pause*]

I don't know what she's going to do next. I mean what in god's name does she want? When you think you've got her pinned you haven't. I decided to go into the Academy, oh no, madam has to come. And you wonder why I'm upset. Those snotty bitches, they give you your shitty diploma, all over you like a bad case of hives, and one week later it's looking right through you. 'We've written personnel the letter, Barbie. Don't you think that's the best we can do. And sent them a copy of your diploma. And we spent a lot of time making your resume look'. . . 'Look what?', I said, 'Look like I've been someone?' I might write to them myself. And I'll hand-deliver. And how do I know where to deliver it? [*This hurts. She hands* DEN *a crushed piece of newspaper which he reads.*] Currently conducting interviews. Currently. Team for our hotel. All positions. Blah blah blah chef, blah blah blah [*Crying*] Hostesses. Opportunity for advancement. Preference to locals. Oh god, this is serious. Why haven't I heard.

DEN: They've got all your info, you're probably on top of the pile.

[*Pause*]

Eh, you weren't wearing that outfit, were you? When you went in there.

BARBARA: So?

DEN: It's just. . .

BARBARA: Well what? What is it? What does it matter? I couldn't go in. I couldn't go up the stairs. She follows me there. Won't wait outside. I can't take her in like any normal sub-normal. Because every time I talk to someone she says, This is my mother who deserted me but now we're back together again.

[*Pause*]

I need help. I'm falling apart. Bits of me are falling off all over the place and before I get a chance to turn around and pick them up some fucking, some fucking, twelve-ton lorry drives right over them.

DEN: Come to bed. I'll give you that back-rub.

BARBARA: It's five o'clock.

[*Pause*]

Don't you know anything? Only very common people fuck in the afternoons. And Lotto closes at six.

[BARBARA *grabs all her papers and moves off.*]

DEN: [*catching her*] Something I should have told you ages ago. I mean, I don't know if it matters. My sister actually owns this house.

[BARBARA *stops, does not look at him, and continues off.*]

Sounds of the fabrication shop floor – welding, clanking of cranes – DEN *moves to pick up his broom and shovel.* DEN *begins to sweep and shovel silver blue metal shearings.* RON *enters and stands some distance away. The tuba plays, as dissonant as the machinery. After a few moments,* DEN *realises that* RON *is there. He is pleased to see him.*

DEN: Start missing the devon sandwiches?

[RON *smiles*]

RON: [*calling*] Can't keep away.

[DEN *stops work and examines his shovel.*]

DEN: [*calling*] I've decided not to part company with this. I'm going to have it mounted – good thing it's already stuffed so that's something taken care of.

[RON *joins him, smiling and looking around as he does so.*]

RON: Listen – I wanted –

[*Momentarily interrupted by a loud noise.*]

I wanted to tell you myself. I shouldn't even be in here. Just look like nothing's going on.

DEN: That's how I usually look.

RON: They're selling it off. Here. The government.

[*Pause*]

To Davis and Dixon.

[*Silence*]

DEN: Privatising?

RON: If you like. . .

[*Pause*]

DEN: A private mob couldn't be any worse.

[*Pause*]

Be a bit hungrier, I've always thought that.

[*Pause*]

Wouldn't they make more of a go of this China business –

RON: All we've been doing is smartening the place up for a sale. The bastards knew they were going to sell. Before we even walked in here. Just wanted us to pave the way.

DEN: Oh, your pride's hurt. Never mind, you're meant to leave that at the gate.

[RON *kicks some of the shearings.*]

RON: Braddon and his ten year speech. 'An unequivocal assurance'. . .

DEN: That's right. Can't go back on that.

[*Pause*]

We all heard that.

[*Pause*]

There'd be a contract out on him if he went back on that – everyone here'd chip in.

RON: Davis and Dixon won't be operating from here.

[*Pause*]

DEN: We'd have to move up there?

RON: They don't want two sites. They'll take the foundry, some of the contracts, some equipment, and the rest'll go in a fire sale. But Braddon's hands'll be clean.

DEN: I don't understand.

RON: They bought it for the land. Too unproductive this place, not worth investing in.

DEN: But that's not what –

RON: I know – it's been let deteriorate, it could be made tenable, but housing development's a helluva lot easier. Looking out onto the Mediterranean. Braddon hoped a firm'd operate from here but, when all's said and done, the government can't afford to sit on a million dollar site. Basically he's a dickhead.

DEN: The works could move – the union proposed it years –

RON: Forget it. The too-hard basket, this place is already in there.

[*Pause*]

There'll be a redeployment list for other government jobs. That's why I wanted to tell you. I really am very sorry.

DEN: What government jobs? There aren't any left. When the power station closed they either came here or a couple of dozen got jobs as cleaners in a prison.

[*Pause*]

[*Quietly*] This can't be happening.

RON: The closure's to be quick and quiet and in four weeks, with no adverse publicity. You're not headed for martyrdom, there'll be the usual package. I just wanted to tell you myself. I better go.

DEN: I trusted you.

RON: [*looking around*] I trusted myself. Isn't it just what the country needs – another few hundred highly-skilled cab-drivers?

DEN: You don't know this area any more. People who are forty, fifty – you don't get taken on.

RON: There'll be something. You've got –

DEN: Fifty-year-olds have regular benches in shopping malls. With eighteen-year-olds. The ones who haven't done themselves in.

RON: I just wanted to tell you because that list for redeployment won't be a long one.

DEN: I'd still be classified a labourer.

RON: He who pays the piper mate. If they can find you a job, take it. You've been doing it this long.

DEN: You didn't have to tell me my job was going to be different.

RON: Don't think I feel particularly victorious, we've been shafted too.

DEN: That there was some chance that we might stop dreading coming in here. Have some sort of say. That we all might find some parts of our minds that we've forgotten how to use.

[*He flings the shovel down to* RON.]

RON: If anyone saw that, you just say a family tiff.

DEN: I can't keep doing this –

RON: Then you take the money. What the hell do you think they should do – offer you an engineering degree?

DEN: I won't take any package. I won't take the money.

[RON *throws the shovel back to* DEN, *who catches it.*]

RON: Yes well, we've all heard that before. What a bloody silly thing to say.

[RON *leaves.* DEN *takes a scoop of shearings. The light catches them as they fly through the air.* BARBARA *runs in under them.* VERGE *watches her mother, endeavouring to join in.*]

BARBARA: Oh you beauty. Oh you beauty. Oh. [*She holds out her arms, and lifts her face to the sky as if she is catching rain.*] Send it down – soak me in the stuff – I've never been more ready in my entire life.

[VERGE *imitates* BARBARA.]

We're rich, we're rich, we're rich, we're rich. We're rich. I hope that doesn't sound a bit greedy.

[DEN *watches her. He remains at a distance from her throughout the scene.*]

[*to* DEN] You beauty. Weeeeeeee! You beauty. . .

VERGE: Weeeeeeeee! Weeeeeee!

[VERGE *turns on the spot, watching her skirt fly out, and then runs to hug her mother.*]

DEN: Come inside.

BARBARA: Lump-sum. Golden, golden handshake. A-little-somethin-to-keep-you-going. Tide-you-over. Thousands, bloody thousands. [*Pointing to* DEN] I knew you. I had you spotted. I knew you'd come up with something. Just when I'd given up on those bastards who can't even reply to letters. Who can't see dedication staring them in the face. Well, that's all behind me. It's a relief actually. Still, I've come out of it all with some skills, [*To* VERGE, *who agrees*] haven't I? Marketable skills.

[*Pause*]

Never ever in my entire life has the right thing happened at the right time. True. I've always been patting a flying bird. Well, we'll catch it this time, even if we have to whack it on the head with a hammer.

[*Pause*]

Plan B. Oh, Den. I had this idea but I kept it to myself because I didn't think it was possible. Don't you want to know?

DEN: Come inside please.

BARBARA: No-one can see me.

DEN: They can hear you.

[*A very loud coal truck rumbles up the hill.*]

BARBARA: You deserve this Den. I deserve it. Everybody deserves it – but who's got it? Us.

DEN: [*quietly*] It isn't even a year's wages.

BARBARA: Eh? [*She comes closer.*]

DEN: It's not a golden handshake, Barbara. It's not enough to live on for a year.

BARBARA: Money's not to live on. It's just to use so you can get more. I do know Den. I have been thinking about money pretty solidly for most of my waking life.

VERGE: Is it gold? Is it? What is it?

DEN: [*to himself. Holding his head*] This is. . . I must be going mad. [*To* BARBARA] I can't take that payout.

BARBARA: You don't take it. They just give it to you. They don't ask you. Blind Freddie knows they don't ask you. This couldn't come at a better time. Or do you mean you can't take it because it's not enough.

DEN: Tell me who I am. What you see?

BARBARA: God you say some strange things.

VERGE: Den!

BARBARA: [*pushing* VERGE] Go for a walk. I'm telling you to go for a walk. [*Sarcastically to* DEN] Tell me who i am. . .

VERGE: [*answering the question*] You're this person –

BARBARA: You're as bad as him, get out of it –

VERGE: Who likes trains.

BARBARA: Dear god in heaven will you disappear. Go!

> [VERGE *goes. Pause.* BARBARA *decides to change tack.*]
> Now, come on cheer up. Have you any idea. Any idea what we could do with that money? Because I have, Sunny Jim. Go three kilometres east, and you get to a resort hotel which is already booked out with conferences, everything. What do people do on conferences. I'm not stupid, they go to the beach. What do you see when you go to Resort Beach?

DEN: City. City Beach.

BARBARA: Apart from a lot of people – fuck all. Sand. And what's the council calling for? Tenders. And what do you need to tender? Money. I've been thinking about it for ages. People have needs. They need umbrellas. They need surfie planes. They need every conceivable item to help them float. They need windbreaks. We could do that. We could be in on that.

> [*Silence*]
> It's what people do when they get retrenched. Use the dough to set themselves up and never look back. Keep flying through, fuck you all and thanks for the memories.

DEN: Barbara –

BARBARA: I am telling you – people need windbreaks on that beach.

DEN: I'm not an entrepreneur.

BARBARA: Well you have to be.

DEN: I don't know a thing about business.

BARBARA: Well you have to. People have to look after themselves. That's the solution.

DEN: Is that the answer to all our problems? Seventeen thousand entrepreneurs. Sixteen thousand fish and chip shops, and a few concessions on the beach?

BARBARA: Who cares? Who cares? It's the answer to ours.

DEN: It's a payment to be quiet. To go out on tip-toes.

BARBARA: So? That's what they've always paid you for.

DEN: We could still make a go of things –

BARBARA: I don't get you. How can you do this to me? All right, all right. You want a baby? You need money to have a baby, don't you? What do you think they eat – grass cuttings or something? Don't even think of doing this. Please. Things just keep – slipping. . .

DEN: It wouldn't even be one year's pay.

BARBARA: Jesus, we're just lucky they don't line us up against a wall and chop off all our heads when they want to get us out of the way. No – they say sorry and shove a cheque in our hands.

[DEN *starts to leave.* VERGE *runs in.*]

No-one does this! This is not what people do! There's no decision to be made! Don't you think you deserve to have a life? [*To* VERGE] Buzz off. Buzz off.

DEN: It's all right. . .

BARBARA: [*to* DEN] Do you mind? [*To* VERGE] Clear out or I'll chop your head off.

[VERGE *goes.* BARBARA *moves to* DEN *as he begins to walk up the hill.*]

All right. You've just worked out that they're a pack of bastards. They're prize shits, never to be trusted – but this is not the time to tell them. You think whether you deserve to have a life.

[BARBARA *leaves.*]

DEN *looks behind him, and scrambles up a hill. There is a sound of passing cars.* RON *is in pursuit.*

RON: Tell me, you tell me.

> [*They stop.*]

DEN: It hasn't got anything to do with you.

RON: You want to know what your choices are? You either take the money and go. Or go. By the time you wake up to yourself their cheque book'll be well and truly shut.

> [RON *starts to circle* DEN.]

You see I won't let you do this to me. I will not have you on my conscience. You're a cost and they're cutting costs. Well, bad luck. We're all servants of accountancy – they might end up with a work force of one but by god their ratio'll be looking healthy, but it's their prerogative because they're the ones running a business, not you. Not me. And I suppose you'd be the only one who's ever had it hard.

DEN: [*tired*] It isn't anything to do with you.

RON: I'm smirked at by every conscientious young prick who's ever walked in the door of my firm, because my degree's not posh enough. And they've shafted us, but we're still getting paid. What you're doing is financial suicide. You're shooting yourself in the arse with Barbara, I can guarantee you that.

DEN: When you're never told what's going on. If two years ago they'd come on the floor –

RON: And levelled with you that they were intending to sell and get the place geared up – yeah all right, that's what sophisticated management'd do, I agree, but you've got a few big bunnies running this show.

DEN: Whose fault's that?

RON: I love this. Let's not harbour any illusions, mate – you've been party to this for twenty-five years. You're a recidivist with the best of them. Don't blame Davis and Dixon – why would they take on a touchy, moody, badly organised work force peering out of blankets of cynicism?

DEN: Is that what you wrote?

RON: Other members of my consultancy did get the impression that you've got blokes who'd still be arguing demarcation while they were being lowered into their graves. Not to mention the morons upstairs –

DEN: When all you're trying to do is hold on –

RON: You know what the truth is. This is the sort of event one plans for. One anticipates. You don't just hold on. When the ground's cracking from under you, you predict where the crevices'll appear and leap onto the next safe patch. Stand there gaping and you're on your own without any water.

[*Pause*]

I'd be asking myself why I didn't ever demand to know what was going on.

DEN: You tell me what you were doing here.

RON: A job. My job.

DEN: I reckon it's a racket.

RON: That's right, that's why we've got work lined up for the next five years. People with billion dollar enterprises ask us for assessments. That's right, it's all a racket. The bottom line is you were unlucky enough to work on a site that's got spectacular views.

DEN: [*continuing with his train of thought*] The government'd be pleased with this result. I reckon there'd be a few more contracts in the pipeline for you. Here's what I think you do. You crank up performance a bit, then they want the problems down on paper, and you ask us what the problems are and then go and tell them. I could have done that. And everyone reads it and says, 'yep, just as we expected. Workers, equipment. . . too far gone'. Yes, you analyse the shit out of a place.

RON: Everything's a risk.

DEN: You don't take risks, you're like the person on the beach who sees someone in a rip, takes his shoes off, jumps up and down and hopes he looks like he's about to dive in.

[*Silence*]

RON: Get this very clear. We were here to undertake cultural change and we got used. I ought to frogmarch you all the way up there and hold your hand while you sign it and in a few weeks time you'd be grateful.

[*Pause*]

Jeannie'll still sell the house. Probably quickly before the rest of the street does.

[BARBARA *enters, from a dimly lit corner as he goes.*]

Remember what your old man used to say about mining – it's dark, and you look after your own light.

[*Pause*]

No-one else is going to do it for you.

DEN's *house.* BARBARA *brings with her a trail of panty-hose, make-up, beauty case etc. She has been crying. Clothes and hair awry.* DEN *goes to her. She is savagely wiping make-up off her diploma.*

BARBARA: You don't just barge in! Barging in when people are . . . Well, have your laugh. It's the bloody diploma. Covered in Ivory Rose or Just Peaches or whatever the hell it is.

DEN: Where is she? Where's Verge?

BARBARA: Went mad and I shot her. Out, out. She's out.

[*She continues to scratch at the diploma.*]

[*reading through the make-up*] Now it looks like 'hospital' industry not hospitality. Why aren't you at work? Kakanno mono Kimasu. Which means get out before I chuck something.

[BARBARA *begins to try on pair after pair of panty-hose. Some she checks before she puts them on, but they've all got holes and ladders.*]

DEN: I've decided. I want you to –

BARBARA: Nothing to do with me.

DEN: Well, it is.

BARBARA: No sorry. Not for me. Will he, won't he. Not all this. Not for me. [*The panty-hose*] Dear god in heaven.

DEN: Because it's selling my job away. It should be the last resort.

BARBARA: Well it is. It is the last resort. Tell you what – don't go sticking your neck out in search of the end of the track . . . I'd say you'll find that you're on it.

DEN: There'll be something else.

BARBARA: Oh not for you. Not for the man who's not even interested in claiming what's due. Any opportunity leaps up and bites you on the nose you drop dead of shock.

[*She struggles with the panty-hose.* DEN *watches.*]

DEN: Where do you have to go?

[*Pause*]

Just cut one leg off one and one off the other. . .

BARBARA: Oh, sure! Then I'd be wearing a double-gussett. Oh, lovely. You wear a double-gusset and see how relaxed you feel.

DEN: I love you. That's the first thing.

BARBARA: Hah!

DEN: If I just knew I had your –

BARBARA: Nothing. You can have nothing from me.

DEN: Support. It's the principle.

BARBARA: The only principal I know said I was stupid and if I smoked my tits'd stop growing.

DEN: You're not stupid. I think –

BARBARA: You can think that I'm a mermaid. I don't care. [*The panty-hose*] Jesus wept.

DEN: This closure shouldn't have happened. It's a matter of living with myself.

BARBARA: Well you got one wish, you will be living with yourself.

DEN: I can't explain –

BARBARA: Bullshit you can't explain. You've done fuck-all for twenty-five years and the day the bosses decide to give you what is fair, and legal and – coincides with the day you think you might just fart in their faces.

[*Pause.*]

I was starting to feel safe!

[BARBARA *throws some things on the ground. And continues with her make-up.*]

DEN: I'll look after you somehow.

BARBARA: I knew you were strange. Very strange for a man. That's what I thought at first. Butter wouldn't melt in your mouth – next up it's a screaming belly-flop onto the slag-heap. Don't you even think about me.

DEN: Where are you going?

BARBARA: [*continuing with her make-up*] You see, I'm not just interested in taking up space. A bit of something for the air to go around. All right they overlooked me. But I'm worth an interview. I deserve to be given a chance. There are sheilas worse than me working there, I've seen them. Why not me? I'm not like you, I forgive.

DEN: I won't let you go. Not dressed like that. [*Grabbing her*] You don't go to the hotel dressed like that.

[*Pause*]

I will not have you laughed at. I don't know if you notice – maybe you don't –

BARBARA: [*backing away*] Poison. You're poison.

[*She blocks her ears with her hands and sings.*]

DEN: Look at yourself.

[*He prizes her arms away.*]

People have started staring at you in the streets.

BARBARA: Because they're jealous.

DEN: Your face is running.

BARBARA: Well, of course they all admire you. What you're doing'll have everyone gasping for air. I don't think.

DEN: You look like you've been in a – disaster. . .

BARBARA: I have!

DEN: A flood – I can't even see you.

BARBARA: I must have been mad. I was getting along so well –

DEN: No!

BARBARA: I knew I didn't need another bloke but oh no, I felt sorry for you.

DEN: I met you dragging boxes through the gateway of a boarding house. And what did I say to you? What did I say to you? You were alone, dying on your feet, dragging garbage bags through the gate –

BARBARA: Shut up.

DEN: And I asked you if you were in the right place. I said were you sure, and I didn't like to point it out but this looks more like a hostel for single men. Just when I was thinking maybe she's a hooker, you said, 'Just 'til I get on my feet'. And you smiled. You had a very nice smile. I used to be able to see you in it. If this is on your feet. . . You go to that hotel, and they'll never see you again. They'll snigger when you leave. A tired old tart with illusions of something else.

BARBARA: If that's what you think why'd you keep on encouraging me?

[*Pause*]

We can't answer, can we?

DEN: I thought it would make you happy.

[*Pause*]

I thought it was what you wanted to hear.

[VERGE *appears. Her hands are tied behind her back, and she's gagged. A truck passes.* DEN *runs to her and unties her.*]

What are you. . . it's all right. . .

[VERGE *stands and stares at her mother.*]

VERGE: [*to* BARBARA] See, I could so get out of that cupboard. [*To* DEN] She thought she'd locked me in.

BARBARA: I'm late.

[DEN *blocks* BARBARA *and has to stop himself from hitting her.*]

I'm late.

DEN: [*slowly*] You tell me this was some kind of joke.

BARBARA: [*to* VERGE] Because you follow me! [*To* DEN] You try telling her she has to stay home. Over and over and over and over. You stand at the bus stop and plead with her not to get on.

DEN: This is your child.

BARBARA: I know. [*To* VERGE] I know you're my daughter. . .

VERGE: I just wanted to go and vouch for her.

[BARBARA *goes to* VERGE, *and holds her face.*]

BARBARA: [*exhausted*] For what! For what? Vouch for me –
wouldn't that be just what I needed. I'm late.

[DEN *blocks her way.*]

VERGE: That she could do the job!

BARBARA: God!

DEN: Let her speak.

VERGE: [*crying*] Whatever it is.

[BARBARA *starts to back* VERGE *into a corner.*]

BARBARA: For god's sake would you even know? Have you any
idea what you're talking about?

VERGE: [*crying and running to* DEN] No!

[BARBARA *looks at* VERGE *and* DEN.]

BARBARA: So chummy. Aren't we so chummy? Quite a team.
Met your match. Verge, you don't find Den boring do you?
Not like Mummy does. Uncle Den doesn't bore you to tears.

DEN: Don't use her. Don't.

[*She searches for the cruellest thing she can think of.*]

BARBARA: Oh well, why not? Don't you? Don't you wop it up
her from time to time?

[DEN *starts to swipe at* BARBARA *who dodges.*]

Not that she'd notice because it's pretty bloody small. Hah!
One more thing that's boring.

[DEN *realises what he's doing and stops.*]

Because isn't he just the most clapped out old fuck?

[BARBARA *gathers up what she can and backs out.*]

Take their money!

Hooter. Sounds of the fabrication shop floor. VERGE *clings to*
DEN, *as she watches* BARBARA *leave. They run from the house,
quickly grabbing a tin of petrol on the way. They sneak onto the
fabrication shop floor. Lights change. The hooter sounds.*

DEN: [*to* VERGE] Sit there. Please don't move. Keep your eyes
down, and don't do a single thing unless I tell you.

[DEN *climbs onto something from which he can be seen
and raises his voice to speak to others on the floor.*]

If all of you wouldn't mind – for a sec – if you could just
listen – I wanted to say something before I go. If you could
just listen –

[*Machines start up.*]

I'm not just some mad bastard who cracked up. But I have
just formally refused the retrenchment package.

[*More machines start up, deliberately drowning him out.*
VERGE *has a scoop of sharp metal shearings in her hand.*]

And I will be heard! Look! Look!

[*He holds aloft the tin of petrol and flings it in a circle
around himself.*]

This is petrol! Petrol! So – just stand still, please. And listen.

[*He holds a cigarette lighter.* VERGE *is curled up,
trying to block everything out. The machines begin to
stop.*]

Because I will have my say. Because this will keep
happening. Because we're one more thing that gets disposed
of – and I keep thinking, what do they think I am? And the
point is, there were people who were paid to plan, to win
contracts, to stop the rust. If the writing was on the wall why
wasn't it read out loud? Look, I know I'm thick, but this
accountancy, all this accountancy – where are the people in
their equations? It's all rates of return and – [*Brandishing
the lighter*] Just stand still or I will do this! We're not stupid
– we could be told the truth. But it's just deceit and –

[VERGE *has extended one arm, and is slowly slashing at
it, watching the blood drip. She is hidden from* DEN.]

The money this region's produced – and it doesn't seem to
get back here. All around us these companies – making these
profits but it all gets spent on expanding in Chile or North
Sea oil or one bad year and they go. And we – we put up
with it.

VERGE: Den.

[*An emergency siren sounds in the distance.*]

DEN: [*not hearing* VERGE] We're like some cargo cult, all of us in this city. Sitting on the floor of a quarry, lighting fires and hoping someone'll come down and save us.

[*The siren continues,* VERGE *is slowly getting to her feet.* DEN *is starting to flounder.*]

Then you wonder – well, what if no-one does? [*Getting softer*] If they think we'll just. . . disappear. . .

[*He looks down, still searching for words.*]

VERGE: [*calling weakly*] Tell them Den. . . you have to. . .

[*Pause*]

DEN: Anyway. . . it's. . . it's water, it's only water. . .

[*He holds up the lighter and flicks it on. Then shrugs, he has had his say and turns to* VERGE. *But she is standing, blood dripping down her arms.*]

VERGE: [*to* DEN] Not worth doing unless it's worth doing well...

[*She extends her bloodied arms out to him.* DEN *freezes. Then he runs to her, picks her up, and goes. As he does, machinery starts up and the sound of the siren gets closer. Then all sounds die.*]

Dusk on the hill. BARBARA *waits up there. It is quiet.* DEN *arrives.* BARBARA *barely looks at him. Sound of gulls, music.*

DEN: I got your note.

BARBARA: Well, I wasn't coming in.

[*Pause*]

Where's Verge?

DEN: She's safe. With Marj. Just for the time being. We all decided.

BARBARA: I bet.

[*Pause*]

Well anyway I'm off on a cruise around the Pacific.

DEN: I don't believe that.

[*Pause*]

BARBARA: You take back all those things you said about me.

DEN: I can't.

[*Pause*]

BARBARA: Anyway it's all in the past. Put it all behind me. Would never have worked. Certainly not for me. There's a bloody great world out there. I was just thinking about these ferry trips we used to get taken on to Manly. When we were little. I like boats. And how at the end of the wharf there used to be these boys, teenage boys, diving off the high part for coins. Silver coins. Sixpences and shillings. And how sometimes someone'd trick them. You know throw in a penny. And one of them'd go in. Just as straight as if it was a shilling. [*To* DEN] Not me. I won't. Diving for dirty old pennies.

DEN: We've both done a bit of that.

[*Pause*]

BARBARA: When you think how we could have been. . . diving for anything. . . pearls. . .

[*Slight pause.* DEN *starts to go.*]

Just for the time being. With Marj. What's that supposed to mean?

DEN: When everything's settled she's to come down to me.

BARBARA: She can look after herself.

DEN: Just as she'd prefer.

BARBARA: Well there's a very big For Sale sign out the front of your place.

DEN: Yes.

[BARBARA *has one last look at him and begins to move down the hill.*]

BARBARA: When everything's settled. Won't that be the day.

[DEN *watches her leave. Lights fade.*]

THE END

Also From Currency

In Our Town Jack Davis

'Somebody once said love knows no barrier. I would like to add, neither does racism' wrote Jack Davis in his program note for the first production of *In Our Town*. Love is at the centre of this drama, as two young men return from fighting side-by-side in the Second World War, but discover that their close friendship cannot be maintained in peacetime. The status quo is changing and the people of their town feel threatened. Racism flares when David, a hero in war, falls in love with Sue, a white woman.

88pp. 8 b/w photographs. Introductions by Adam Shoemaker, Lecturer, Departme of Humanities, Queensland University of Technology and by Lynette Narkle, ac in all of Jack Davis's previous plays and assistant director of this production. Teacl resource notes on the play will be available in 1993.

Hotel Sorrento Hannie Rayson

Hilary lives in seaside Sorrento with her father and sixteen-year-old son; Pippa visiting from New York and Meg returns from England with her English husbar Three sisters, reunited after ten years in different worls, again feel the constraints family life. It is Meg's semi-autobiographical novel, recently short-listed for t Booker prize, which overshadows their homecoming.

104pp. 8 b/w photographs. Introductions by director Aubrey Mellor and the autho Teacher resource notes on the play will be available in 1993.

Diving for Pearls Katherine Thomson

The story of two ordinary people discarded by the lean, mean 90s world. As a gloss resort grows in place of the old community of steel-workers, Barbara and Den mal sometimes incongruous attempts to adjust to the new demands of the times. Barbar doggedly optimistic, Den painfully resentful, together assault the unfamili heartlessness in outbursts of emotional power and with a stubborn humour weath the chaos around them.

104pp. 8 b/w photographs. Introductions by Di Kelly, Economics Departmen University of Wollongong and Paul Thompson, Head of Scriptwriting, Australian Film Television and Radio School. Teacher resource notes on the play will be available in 1993.

St James Infirmary Nick Enright

A student about to sit for his HSC at a Catholic boys' school, stages an anti-Vietnam protest. In the infirmary, he has to face the issues of personal and public responsiblity.

96pp. 8 b/w photographs. Introductions by novelist Gerard Windsor and director George Ogilvie. Teacher resource notes will be available.

Currency Press, PO Box 452, Paddington 2021, Australia.
Tel (02) 332 1300. Fax (02) 332 3848.